BIBLE IN BRIEF

An easy way to enjoy
the greatest book
ever written

Rev Andy Roland

Published by Filament Publishing Ltd
16, Croydon Road, Waddon, Croydon Surrey CR0 4PA

The right of Andrew Roland to be identified as the author of this work
has been asserted by him in accordance with the
Designs and Copyright Act 1988

© Andrew Roland 2016 Illustrations by Daniel Gould

Printed by Ingram Spark ISBN 978-1-910819-86-9

The book is protected by international copyright and may not
be copied in anyway without the prior written permission
of the publishers.

Table of Contents

Introduction		5
How to use this book		9
Using the book with a group		10
The Bible - a bird's eye view		15

Month 1   **CREATION TO COMMANDMENTS**   **20**

- Week 1   Beginnings   22
- Week 2   Abraham, Isaac, Jacob   26
- Week 3   Joseph & the move to Egypt   30
- Week 4   The Desert Experience   34
- The Other Side: Stories from Babylon   38
- Creation and Flood   40

Month 2   **HISTORY OF ISRAEL & JUDAH**   **42**

- Week 1   Prophetic leaders & the first king   44
- Week 2   David and Solomon   48
- Week 3   Divided Kingdoms   52
- Week 4   Exile & Restoration   56
- The Other Side: Rival Empires   60

Month 3   **THE PROPHETS**   **64**

- Week 1   The Fall of Israel   68
- Week 2   The Fall of Judah   72
- Week 3   Speaking from Babylon   76
- Week 4   Hope and Disappointment   80
- The Other Side: Prayers of the Peoples   84

Month 4	**LAW, PSALMS & WISDOM**	**88**
	Week 1 The Law	90
	Week 2 Devotional Psalms	94
	Week 3 Psalms and Sayings	96
	Week 4 Suffering and futility	100
	The In between	104
Month 5	**JESUS**	**114**
	Week 1 Starting up and teaching	116
	Week 2 The mission intensifies	122
	Week 3 The final challenge	126
	Week 4 John's Gospel	130
	The Other Side: Jewish Schools of Thought	134
Month 6	**APOSTLES & THEIR LETTERS**	**142**
	Week 1 Acts of the Apostles	144
	Week 2 Paul's letter to new Christians	148
	Week 3 Paul's letter to Christians in Rome	152
	Week 4 Other letters	156
	The Other Side: Roman Reactions	162

BONUS FEATURES

The World's Greatest Book?	166
Chapter and Verse	169
Which Bible?	170
Scientists on the Bible	173
Film recommendations	174
Illustrations	179
What has been missed out?	181
Andy Roland - a brief biography	182

Introduction

When I was at university, I made a new commitment of my life to God. For me that involved a new wish to study the Bible.

A particular help to me then was a small green paperback, published by the Bible Reading Fellowship in 1957, entitled "Seeing the Bible Whole" by Stephen Neill. It gave an overview of the Bible in four months: two months for the Old Testament and two for the New. Each passage had a page of commentary. It was a great way to get to grips with the whole Bible.

Sadly it is now out of print. As far as I know, nothing has replaced it as a way of giving an overview of the Bible in the Bible's own words.

This booklet is offered as an attempt to fill the gap. It is offered primarily to two kinds of readers:

- those who want to read the Bible for the first time but don't know where to start. Many start at Genesis 1 and get bogged down in Exodus with the ten plagues of Egypt and the exhaustive description of the Tabernacle or Tent of Meeting with its "blue, purple and scarlet stuff and fine twined linen". The aim of this book is to give an overview of the Bible, including most of the famous stories, showing where they fit in to the whole.

- The book is also for Christians who would like to get to know the Bible better, or who know part of the Bible quite well, usually the gospels, but would like a way into the less familiar parts like the Old Testament prophets.

Each month has its own overarching theme, and each week can be used as self-contained set of readings, for example, the reigns of David and Solomon, (Month 2, week 2).

You absolutely do not need to start from the beginning and go on to the end, though I hope it will make sense if you do so. Start at something that grabs your attention or curiosity and you can then read backwards or forwards from that point. 1t is probably helpful to take a complete week at a time.

The Other Side

You will also see that at the end of each month's readings there is a section called "The Other Side". These are writings from the surrounding cultures of the time. It can really help our understanding of the Bible if we can place the Jewish and Christian scriptures in the wider overall context.

- After Genesis and Exodus there are extracts from the the Babylonian stories of the Creation and the Flood.
- After the history section there are quotations from the Assyrian and Babylonian annals
- After the section on the prophets come examples of prayers from the nations surrounding Israel.

The prophets also spoke against the worship of Baal. Until an ancient temple was excavated in Ras Shamra in northern Syria around 1930 nothing was known about it. Now we have a long poem about the death and resurrection of Baal as a fertility god, from which I quote a few stanzas, and other prayers from the nations surrounding Israel.

- There is a gap of about 400 years between the end of the Old Testament as most people know it and the New Testament. It included the Maccabean Revolt of 167 BC in which Israel amazingly defeated the mighty Seleucid empire and became a self-governing state for over 100 years. A contemporary account is given in the fourth section, together with other passages from the same time.

- In the New Testament, a lot is said criticising the Pharisees. It is instructive to read some of the things the Pharisees actually said; as well as contemporary accounts of other Jewish parties. These make it clear how scandalous Jesus must have seemed in the eyes of many of his contemporaries.

- Finally, after the letters from the Early Church we have examples of what the normal Romans really thought of this new sect - not good.

The main virtue, I believe, we need in approaching the Bible – or indeed religious scriptures and faith in general – is curiosity. Don't be afraid to explore.

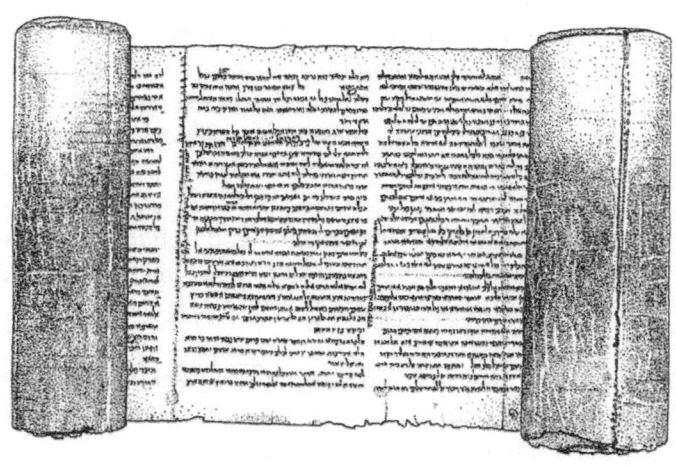

Isaiah scroll from the Dead Sea Scrolls

How to use this book

To get the most out of this book, you can use the 4 Rs:

READ   **RESPOND**   **REFLECT**   **RECORD**

Read
- You can read through the passage once, then look back at any particular verses that interest you;
- or you can read it through quickly once and slowly a second time;
- or you can read it slowly, pausing at any verse that speaks to you;
- or just read it anyway you like!
- Read any explanatory notes that are provided.

How you read any particular passage depends on the type of story it is and how you relate to it. There is no "one size fits all".

Respond
- Note down what bits of the passage impress you, or inspire you, or puzzle you, or infuriate you.
- Don't worry about parts of the passage which leave you bewildered.
- Concentrate on the bits that make sense to you and leave the rest for later – maybe much much later!

Reflect
- Reflect on the question provided in the text.

Record
- Write down your response to the question. Over time you will build up a record of what you have discovered about the Bible and life.

How to use this book - in a group

This book can also be used in small groups. In my last parish we used it in a weekly lunchtime group for a couple of years. The meeting was a cross between Bible meditation and discussion, starting off with some food and drink and ending with a simple form of prayer. You only need four people to get it off the ground and it need not take more than about an hour in total. Here is what we did.

1 Food
Sharing food at the start is crucial to helping people to relax and building up relationships: coffee and biscuits, soup and bread and cheese, tea and cake, even possibly wine and cheese, depending on the time of day you want to meet. It is important to keep the food simple so it does not take over the whole time set for the meeting.

2 Bible
  a) **Reading.** We read the Bible passage set for the day, perhaps each person reading a section, or having it read round the whole group each one taking a verse or two at a time.

  b) **Silence for 5 minutes.** During this time we re-read the passage for ourselves quite slowly, seeing what verse or phrase particularly stands out for us. (Someone needs to be the timekeeper). The time should be set so that people do not start getting anxious, wondering how much longer the silence is going to go on for.

  c) **Reflection.** Each person repeats aloud a verse of phrase which has stood out for them. It is often a moving experience hearing parts of the Bible from

someone else's personal perspective.
Note: this is not the time for venting our own opinions or for general discussion.

d) **Discussion.** Someone introduces the discussion by reading the question and any notes that are linked to the passage. This introduces general discussion for 15 - 20 minutes.

3 Prayer

a) **The Lord's Prayer.** This acts as a transition moment from discussion to prayer. It is good to have available a printed copy of the version you use; nowadays not everyone knows it.

b) **Sharing.** Talk to each other about what and who you might like to pray for. It is helpful to give information directly and so avoid geography-type prayers: "Lord, we pray for our missionaries in Papua/ New Guinea, which, as you know, is just above Australia…"

c) **Teaspoon prayers.** It is helpful to use a teaspoon when praying together. The teaspoon is passed round the group, and whoever has it can then pray aloud - a bit like the Native Americans' pipe of peace. If someone does not want to pray, they simply hand it on to the next person.
Note: We use a teaspoon because it is often shortened in recipes to "tsp", which makes a pretty good formula for prayer, i.e. Thanks, Sorry, Please.

d) **End.** We end by saying the Grace

Additional Prayers

If wanted, there can be a prayer before the Bible reading and at the end of the prayers. We used an Orthodox prayer to the Holy Spirit at the start, and a prayer from the Community of Taize at the end.

Start: Heavenly King, Comforter, Spirit of truth everywhere living, filling all things,
Treasury of good and Giver of life,
come and dwell in us and cleanse us from sin,
and of your goodness, heal our souls.

End: Bless us, Lord, now in the middle of the day.
Be with us and those who are dear to us and with everyone we meet.
Keep us in the spirit of the beatitudes,
joyful, simple, merciful.

The Grace: May the grace of our Lord Jesus Christ,
and the love of God,
and the fellowship of the Holy Spirit,
be with us evermore.
Amen.

Using the website

There is a website to accompany this book, in it you can upload your comments on any of the passages selected in this book, and see what other people have thought about them as well.

www.bibleinbrief.org

Other reading

I don't think I want to recommend too many other books – there is just so much out there, But here are some books which could be useful for further study:

The Bible for Dummies (2002)
Understanding the Bible - John Stott (1978)
The Illustrated Bible – DK (2012)
The Lion Handbook of the Bible (1971)

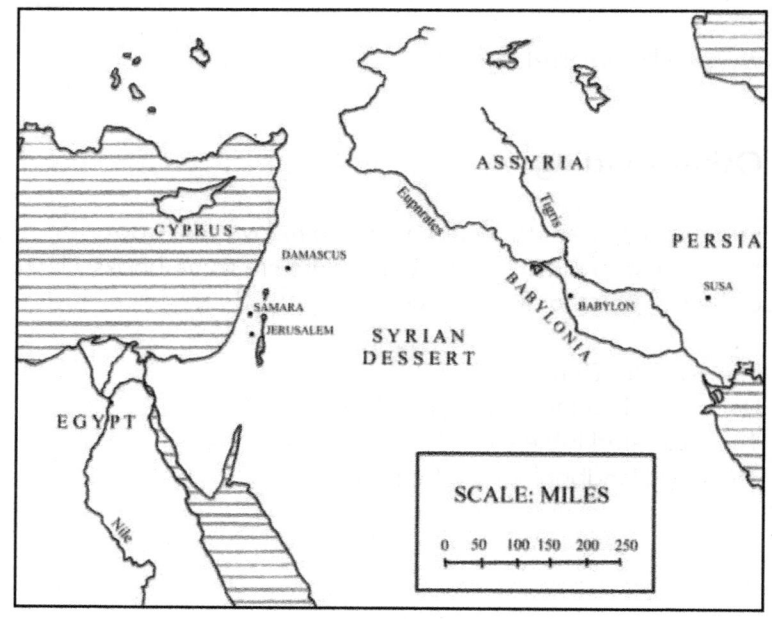

The Ancient Near East

The Bible - A Bird's Eye View

We talk of the Bible as if it were a single book. In fact it is a library. The word Bible comes the Greek 'Biblia' which means books, plural. It includes at least 66 separate writings. The writings were collected in order of types of writing rather than chronologically, so it is quite difficult to get a hang of where to find what. Here is a rough overview.

The Old Testament

This was written in Hebrew between 1000 and 160 BC. It is the holy book of Judaism. Jesus called it "the law and the prophets." Jews call it the "Tenakh" - using the first letters of the Hebrew words for Law, Prophets and Writings. Christians call it the Old Testament – meaning the old covenant – referring to a verse of Paul's in 2 Corinthians 3.14.

> *"The same veil remains (over their minds) when the old covenant is read."*

The Law - The Torah

Genisis, Exodus, Leviticus, Numbers, Deuteronomy
The first five books of the Bible are the fundamental scriptures for Jews. They tell stories of the beginning of the world, of Abraham and his descendants, and of the escape from Egypt. They then record all the laws and regulations given through Moses while the Israelites roamed the wilderness for 40 years.

The Histories

Joshua, Judges, Ruth, 1 & 2 Samuel, 1 & 2 Kings, 1 & 2 Chronicles, Ezra, Nehemiah

These books tell the story of the Israelites from their conquest of the promised land (modern Israel/Palestine) about 1200 BC, to the establishment and destruction of the twin kingdoms of Israel and Judah, and the eventual return of a remnant from exile about 500 BC.

The Writings: Wisdom and Worship

Job, Psalms, Proverbs, Ecclesiastes, The Song of Solomon

This is the personal heart of the Old Testament, where people struggled with questions of life, suffering, success and failure. The psalms are the hymn book of the Jerusalem Temple and offer the whole of life to God – the good, the bad and the ugly.

The Prophets

Isaiah, Jeremiah & Lamentations, Ezekiel, Daniel, "The Twelve"

Prophets were rather fierce individuals who called vigorously for the people of Israel to repent in the years leading up to and following the destruction of Israel and Judah in 622 and 587 BC. Much of their writings are first hand accounts of their messages. They end with a collection of 12 short books written by different prophets at various times.

The Apocrypha

1-4 Macabees, Tobit, Judith, Widom of Solomon, Ecclesiasticus (Sirach), Baruch etc.

The Apocrypha (meaning "hidden") are Jewish writings written in Greek during the two hundred years before Christ. This was because the great majority of Jews lived all over the Roman and Persian worlds rather than in Palestine, and their natural language was Greek. They were taken out of the recognised Jewish scriptures about 100 AD but the Christian church continued to use them. At the time of the Reformation, c.1520-1550, Martin Luther in his translation of the Bible into German, separated the Greek writings into a special section 'The Apocrypha', but they continued to be printed in bibles until 1826 when the National Bible Society of Scotland petitioned the British and Foreign Bible Society to stop printing it.

Most Bibles, apart for Roman Catholic ones, do not include these books. They include uplifting stories and legends, the history of the Maccabean revolt which liberated Jews in Palestine from Persian rule about 165 BC, and wisdom and preaching from that time. A selection has been included after month four.

In Roman Catholic Bibles the books of Samuel and Kings are called Kings 1,2,3 and 4. The numbering of the Psalms also follows the early Greek translation, not the Hebrew one.

The New Testament

This was written in Greek between 50 and 100 AD. The books were chosen as having direct links with the first apostles – Peter, John, Paul etc.

The Gospels

The Gospels are four accounts of the ministry, death and resurrection of Jesus of Nazareth, called Christ or Messiah by his followers. Both Matthew and Luke use Mark as one of the sources of their books. John is quite independent. All were written before 100 AD.

History of the Early Church

The Acts of the Apostles

Luke continues his account of the life of Jesus by telling of the first few years of the Jesus movement in Jerusalem. This is followed by a detailed account of the missionary journeys of Paul to Cyprus, modern Turkey, Greece and ending in Rome around 62AD.

Letters of Paul

Romans, 1 & 2 Corinthians, Galatians, Ephesians, Philippians, Colossians etc.
These are letters from the apostle (missionary) Paul to various congregations in the Roman empire, most of which he had founded. These were usually mixed groups of Jews and non-Jews (Gentiles), a situation which gave rise to many disputes in the early church.

Other letters

Hebrews, James, 1 & 2 Peter, 1, 2 & 3 John, Jude
Letters to the churches in general, from five of the key apostles of the early church.

The Revelation to John

A series of visions given to a church leader in prison for his faith, perhaps around 95 AD. It is similar to contemporary Jewish apocalypses, or visions of the end times.

Note: To find things quickly go to 'Chapter & Verse' in the Bonus Features section on page 169.

MONTH 1
CREATION TO COMMANDMENTS
(Genesis & Exodus)

This month there are three sets of beginnings:
- The world;
- Abraham's faith and family;
- The Hebrew people and religion.

Genesis 1-11 tells stories about the beginning of the world, and the beginning of human society. We do not know when it was written, but it reflects some very early oral tradition.

Some people get hung up on whether modern science contradicts what the Bible says about creation. This betrays a fundamental misunderstanding about the purpose of the biblical accounts. First, there are two accounts, not one. Genesis 1 reflects on the gradual development of the world as seen from a fertile country with access to the sea.
Genesis 2 imagines creation as starting out in a desert land.

Second, the form of Genesis 1 is a poem, not a scientific account. It tells of God creating three stage sets (light and darkness, water and air, land and plants), followed by three groups of actors (sun, moon and stars, birds and fishes, animals and humans). The key concept is that, instead of an eternal conflict between the gods of order and chaos, as in other mythologies, the world which God creates is ordered and "very good".

Month 1: Creation and Commandments

Similarly, whether or not Genesis 3 is an historical event, it certainly is a contemporary one. Archbishop Michael Ramsey was once asked if he believed in original sin. He replied, "Believe in it? I've seen it!"

Whatever the details of Noah's flood, the story may well reflect a major flood or floods in what is modern Iraq about 2900 BC.

In week 2 we step onto the stage of history with the call of Abraham, his direct relationship with God mirroring that of Arab nomads today. We meet his son Isaac, grandson Jacob and great-grandson Joseph.

In week 3 we hear how Joseph was instrumental in bringing his nomadic kinsfolk to settle in north east Egypt for several hundred years, probably while foreigners ruled Egypt. When a native-born Egyptian seized power, the Hebrews became state slaves. A Hebrew, brought up as an Egyptian and called Moses, (an Egyptian name) was commissioned by God to liberate his people.

In week 4 we hear of the escape from Egypt and the nation-building experience of surviving in the desert. The Ten Commandments form the basis of a law-based society.

MONTH 1 WEEK 1
BEGINNINGS

These are stories of primaeval humanity, before history proper. They explore questions like: What is the world like? Why can't people live peaceably? What is the meaning of disasters?

Day 1   Genesis 1 + 2.1-3 The beginning of the world
Is the universe 'good'?
"Made in God's image" - what does this mean?

Day 2   Genesis 2.4-end Beginnings - another account
What do men and women need for life to be good?

Day 3   Genesis 3 Our fall from grace
What attitudes do we have that spoil life?

Day 4   Genesis 4 The first murder
What are the causes and consequences of violence?

Day 5   Genesis 6.9 - 7.end The story of the flood
Note: there were several stories of the flood in the ancient Middle East, reflecting some actual event.
How important is it that a remnant survive a catastrophe?

Month 1: Creation and Commandments

READ **RESPOND** **REFLECT** **RECORD**

In the beginning God created the heavens and the earth.
Genesis 1.1

Day 6   Genesis 8 The end of the flood
Noah's first act on leaving the ark was to worship. Why?

Day 7   Genesis 11.1-9 Humanity disunited
Note: Babel is another name for Babylon, the empire that conquered Judah in 587 BC.
"Pride goes before a fall." Does it?

A Babylonian Ziggurat - mountain temple

Month 1: Creation and Commandments

READ	RESPOND	REFLECT	RECORD

"Whenever the rainbow appears in the clouds,
I will see it and remember the
everlasting covenant between God and
all living creatures of every kind on the earth."
Genesis 9.16

MONTH 1 WEEK 2
ABRAHAM, ISAAC & JACOB c. 1750 – 1600 BC

Day 1 Genesis 12.1-9 The call of Abram
How would it feel to be called into the unknown?

Day 2 Genesis 15 God's promises him a son
Note: Walking between two halves of an animal was the sign of making a solemn covenant (see Jeremiah 34.18)
What do you think Abram felt after his strange encounter with God?

Day 3 Genesis 18.1 – 19.29 The promise to Abraham and the destruction of Sodom
When is it all right to argue with God?

Day 4 Genesis 22.1-19 The test of Abraham's faith
Note: Some ancient cultures practised human sacrifice. (see 2 Kings 3.27).
What did Abraham learn about God and about himself?

Day 5 Genesis 24 Finding a bride for Isaac
Note: Archbishop William Temple (d.1944), when asked if prayer worked, replied, *"I don't know. All I know is that when I pray, co-incidences happen."*
Have you known "God-incidences" in your own life?

Month 1: Creation and Commandments

| READ | RESPOND | REFLECT | RECORD |

Abram believed the LORD,
and he credited it to him as righteousness.
Genesis 15.6

Day 6 Genesis 27 + 28.10-22 Jacob tricks his father and has a dream
What surprising features are there in God's encounter with Jacob, and his response?

Day 7 Genesis 32.3 – 33.11 Jacob's return
What did Jacob's 20 year exile teach him?

Desert Nomads

Month 1: Creation and Commandments

READ **RESPOND** **REFLECT** **RECORD**

"I saw God face to face,
and yet my life was spared."
Genesis 32.30

BIBLE IN BRIEF

MONTH 1 WEEK 3
JOSEPH & THE MOVE TO EGYPT c. 1600 – 1200 BC

Day 1   Genesis 37.1-28 Joseph and his brothers
Did Joseph have it "coming to him"?

Day 2   Genesis 41.1-43 Joseph and Pharaoh's dreams
A spoilt childhood, slavery and prison: a good training to be Prime Minister?

Day 3   Genesis 45 Joseph calls his family to Egypt
"You intended to do me harm, but God intended it for good." (Genesis 50.20)
What was the basis of Joseph's forgiving his brothers?

Day 4   Exodus 1.1 - 2.10 A new king of Egypt
Note: this is 400 years later
What is God's response to the oppression suffered by the Hebrews?

Day 5   Exodus 2.11-25 Moses in exile
Is violence sometimes justified?

Month 1: Creation and Commandments

READ	RESPOND	REFLECT	RECORD

"Do not be distressed...
because it was to save lives
that God sent me ahead of you."
Genesis 45.5

Day 6   Exodus 3 God speaks
What are the two ways that God refers to Him- , Her-, Itself?

Day 7   Exodus 11 God's punishment of Egypt
Death of the eldest child was the climax of the plagues which Egypt suffered when Pharaoh refused to let the Hebrews go. *Why was Pharaoh so stubborn? Is there a parallel with governments now and global warming?*

Egyptian war captives making bricks

Month 1: Creation and Commandments

READ	RESPOND	REFLECT	RECORD

The LORD said,
"I am the God of your father,
the God of Abraham, the God of Isaac
and the God of Jacob."
At this, Moses hid his face, because
he was afraid to look at God.
Exodus 3.6

MONTH 1 WEEK 4
THE DESERT EXPERIENCE:
FORMATION OF A PEOPLE c.1250 – 1200 BC

Day 1   Exodus 12.21-42 The first Passover
What might it mean to a Jewish family each year to celebrate the first Passover?

Day 2   Exodus 14 Crossing the Red Sea
What happened to the sea? (see v.21) How did the Israelites respond?

Day 3   Exodus 16 Bread and meat in the desert
How would you react if you found strange flakes of "bread" on the desert floor?

Day 4   Exodus 19 The people at Mount Sinai
What might it mean to be "a priestly kingdom and a holy nation."

Day 5   Exodus 20.1-17 The Ten Commandments
Do the Ten Commandments make a good foundation for society?
Note: The longer commandments like that on the Sabbath are probably later expansions of the original brief "Ten Words", e.g. "Do not steal".

Month 1: Creation and Commandments

READ   **RESPOND**   **REFLECT**   **RECORD**

"I am the LORD your God,
who brought you out of the land of Egypt,
out of the house of slavery;
you shall have no other gods before me."
Exodus 20.2,3

Day 6   Exodus 33.7 – 34.14 Seeing the Glory
How does God describe himself?

Day 7   Numbers 13 + 14.1-25 Failure of the first attempt to enter Canaan
A missed opportunity. Whose side would you be on and why?
Note: Most of Exodus 21 – 40 is taken up with various laws and regulations, and detailed instructions on how to make the priests' robes and the Tent of Meeting (or Tabernacle). This acted as a movable Temple as the centre of Israel's worship.

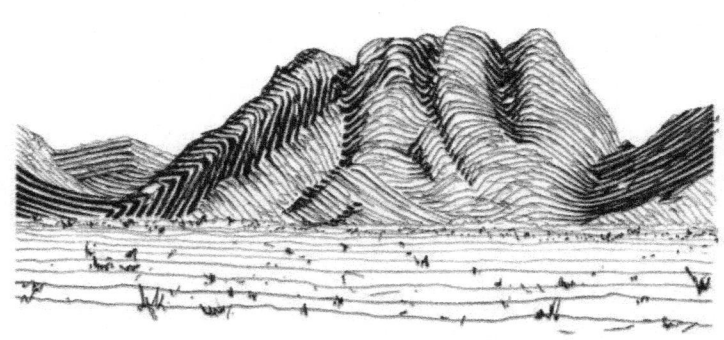

Mount Sinai

Month 1: Creation and Commandments

READ	RESPOND	REFLECT	RECORD

The LORD replied,
"My Presence will go with you,
and I will give you rest."
Exodus 33.14

THE OTHER SIDE
STORIES FROM BABYLON – THE CREATION EPIC

We have a long and complex poem from Babylon, dating about 1750 - 1500 BC, about the time of Abraham, giving their Epic of Creation. Here are a few stanzas:

> *None of the gods had at this time appeared...*
> *In the depths of their waters the gods were created*

But the new gods made too much noise partying, and disturbed the older gods. The goddess Tiamat prepared to destroy them:

> *She unleashed the Irresistible Weapon,*
> *bore monster-serpents.*
> *Sharp was their tooth and pitiless their fang,*
> *with poison instead of blood she filled their bodies.*

However, a new champion for the gods was born, Marduk, the god of Babylon.

> *In the depths of the Apsu*, the god Marduk was born.*
> *He that beget him was Ea, his father...*

Note: Apsu was the watery deep beneath the earth. Tiamat personified the sea. Ea was the god of the sweet waters.

> *So they came together – Tiamat and Marduk,*
> *Sage of the gods.*
> *They advanced into conflict,*
> *they joined forces in battle...*
> *As she opened her mouth, Tiamat, to devour him,*
> *he shot there through an arrow, it tore into her womb...*

Month 1: Creation and Commandments

Thereat he strangled her,
made her life-breath ebb away.
He slit her in two, like a fish in the drying yards.
The one half he positioned and secured as the sky.
There he traced lines for the mighty gods,
stars, star-groups and constellations
he appointed for them...
He placed her head in position,
heaped the mountains upon it,
made the Euphrates and Tigris
to flow through her eyes...

Marduk then planned to build a great city as his palace. The gods object because they think they will have to work too hard looking after it. Marduk has a solution:

Blood I will compose, bring a skeleton into being,
produce a lowly, primitive creature. "Man" shall be his name.
I will create an earthly puppet-man.
To him be charged the service,
that the gods may then have rest...

Note: All the extracts from months 1,2,and 3 are taken from Ancient Near Eastern Texts published by Princeton University Press

Assyrian God Nisroch

STORIES FROM BABYLON
THE GILGAMESH EPIC OF THE FLOOD

The Gilgamesh Epic was composed around 2000 – 1800 BC. Gilgamesh is desperate to find if there was a way for humans to avoid death. In the end he meets the only person to have received eternal life – Uta-pishti – who made a gigantic ark and came safely through the great flood.

The god Ea sent a message to Uta-pishti:

> *"Destroy your house and build a vessel... despising possessions, preserve what has life. Thus load in your vessel the seed of all creatures."*

Uta-pishti obeyed and built a vast wooden cube, sealed with pitch, 120 cubits on each side, with six decks.

> *All that I had I now loaded aboard her... silver... gold...*
> *yea, of the species of all living creatures...*
> *all my family, kindred, beasts, wild and domestic, and all of the craftsmen I made enter the vessel.*
>
> *Swift blew the storm...*
> *it passed over the land like a battle...*
> *Even the gods were afeared at the deluge,*
> *took to flight, and went up to the heaven of Anu*
> *and cowered like dogs.*
>
> *For six days and nights the wind blew,*
> *and the flood and the storm swept the land.*
> *But the seventh day arriving did the rainstorm subside.*
> *I opened a vent ... and I looked at the sea,*
> *the tideway lay flat as a rooftop.*
> *The whole of mankind had returned unto clay.*

Month 1: Creation and Commandments

The ark grounded on Mount Nisar for six days. Uta-pishti sent out first a dove, which returned, then a swallow, which returned, then a raven which did not return.

> *So all I set free to the four winds of heaven,*
> *and I poured a libation, and scattered a*
> *food-offering on the height of the mountain...*
> *The gods smelled the sweet savour,*
> *the gods gathered like flies around the priest of*
> *the offering ...*
>
> *Then Enlil* went up into the vessel.*
> *He took hold of my hand...*
> *and made my wife kneel at my side...*
> *He touched our foreheads and did bless us, saying*
> *"Hitherto, Uta-pishti has been but a man.*
> *But now Uta-pishti and his wife shall be gods like*
> *ourselves..."*

Enlil is the god of air and wind.

Assyrian God Nisroch

MONTH 2
THE HISTORY OF ISRAEL AND JUDAH
1200 – 150 BC

This month we survey the history of the Jewish people from 1200 BC, namely the 650 years when they had their own independent state followed by the 400 years when they were subservient to the mighty empires around them.

First we have two readings which introduce the conquest of Canaan (modern Israel) by the Hebrew tribes, followed by a typical event from the time of the Judges. These were charismatic war leaders who arose from time to time within the tribal confederacy to counter threats from outside.

This anarchic period came to an end when Saul, a tall handsome warrior, was anointed as Israel's first king. His jealousy and insecurities ultimately led to his death at the hands of the Philistines – a warrior people around present day Gaza.

In week 2 we read of the two greatest kings of Israel and Judah – David, a great warrior of mostly noble character and devoted to God; and Solomon his son whose intelligence brought the kingdom to new heights of prosperity, but who also sowed the seed of the break-up of the united monarchy under his own son in 922 BC.

Week 3 gives us snapshots from the 335 turbulent years of the two kingdoms – the wealthy northern kingdom comprising 10 or 11 of the 12 tribes, and the more conservative southern kingdom of Judah with the Temple in Jerusalem.

Month 2: The History of Israel and Judah 1200 - 150 BC

While Israel's monarchy suffered from violent coups d'etat every two or three generations, descendants of David contin- ued to reign in Jerusalem right to the end.

In week 4 we read of the destruction of Jerusalem by Babylon in 587BC, and the Jewish experience of exile and of being a vassal province within the Persian and Seleucid empires. (The latter was set up by one of Alexander the Great's generals in 312 BC on the ruins of the Persian empire). The book of Daniel is thought by many to have been written quite late, around 168 BC, at the time when the Seleucid king was trying to wipe out Judaism. Three brothers, the Maccabees, led a revolt which amazingly defeated the might of the Seleucid empire and Judah became an independent state for the next 100 years. It was at this time, in 103 BC, that Galilee in the north was conquered and re-converted to the Jewish faith.

(The story of the revolt is told in 1 Maccabees, one of the books of the Apocrypha – Jewish writings in Greek which were accepted by the Christian church but not by Jews. At the reformation, c.1520, Martin Luther put these books in a separate section and made them optional reading).
See pages 104-113.

יהוה

MONTH 2 WEEK 1
PROPHETIC LEADERS + THE FIRST KING
c. 1200 – 1000 BC

Day 1   Joshua 1 A new leader
Doing anything worthwhile usually involves struggle. Where is God calling us today to be "strong and courageous"?

Day 2   Joshua 6 The fall of Jericho
Complete destruction of one's enemy was only seen as a sacrifice to God provided none of the attackers profited. Can we reconcile a war crime with obedience to God?

Day 3   Judges 6 + 7 God saves Israel through Gideon
The Israelites were repeatedly attacked by their neighbours. Gideon called them back to their covenant faith, while using guerrilla tactics. What gave Gideon the courage to go on?

Day 4   1 Samuel 8 + 10.20-24 The request for a king
In deciding whether to choose a king rather than Spirit-inspired leaders, what pluses and minuses did the people of Israel consider?

Day 5   1 Samuel 17 David and Goliath
What resources do I have to deal with the Goliaths in my own life? How does God work?

Month 2: The History of Israel and Judah 1200 - 150 BC

READ **RESPOND** **REFLECT** **RECORD**

The LORD was with the men of Judah.
They took possession of the hill country,
but they were unable to drive the people from
the plains, because they had iron chariots.
Judges 1.19

BIBLE IN BRIEF

Day 6   1 Samuel 18.6-11 + Ch.24 David the fugitive
Why did David behave so honourably?

Day 7   2 Samuel 1 David hears of Saul's death
How does David express grief, and how do we?

Canaanite mortuary jars

Month 2: The History of Israel and Judah 1200 - 150 BC

| READ | RESPOND | REFLECT | RECORD |

All the elders of Israel gathered together
and came to Samuel at Ramah.
They said to him, "You are old, and your
sons do not walk in your ways;
now appoint a king to lead us,
such as all the other nations have."
1 Samuel 8.4,5

MONTH 2 WEEK 2
DAVID & SOLOMON c. 1000 – 922 BC

Day 1   2 Samuel 5 David becomes king of all Israel
Note: At the end of a 7 year civil war, David captured Jerusalem as a neutral capital between northern Israel and southern Judah.
What was the secret of David's success?

Day 2   2 Samuel 6 The Ark of the Covenant is brought to Jerusalem
Note: The Ark contained the Ten Commandments
What ways of worship do we recognise? Are there some types that make us feel uncomfortable? Why?
(See also Psalm 132)

Day 3   2 Samuel 11 – 12 David and Bathsheba
Draw a diagram of the actions that David slipped into, leading to his moral downfall – and the steps of his recovery.

Day 4   1 Kings 1 Solomon becomes king 961 BC
Is there anything edifying in this story of a palace coup?

Day 5   1 Kings 3 Solomon's wisdom
How can a person in authority – or any of us — "discern right from wrong"?

Month 2: The History of Israel and Judah 1200 - 150 BC

| READ | RESPOND | REFLECT | RECORD |

When all the elders of Israel had come
to David at Hebron, the king made
a compact with them at Hebron
before the Lord and they anointed
David king over Israel.
2 Samuel 5.3

BIBLE IN BRIEF

Day 6   1 Kings 8.1-40 Dedicating the Temple
What makes places like cathedrals special?

Day 7   1 Kings 12 The nation breaks apart
"Power tends to corrupt, and absolute power tends to corrupt absolutely" (Lord Acton)
What are the temptations of power?

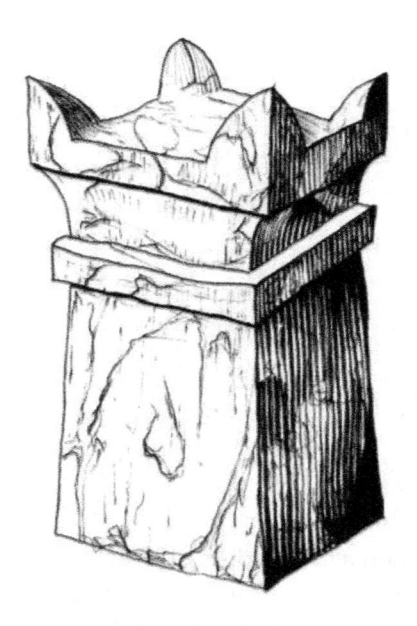

Israelite altar

Month 2: The History of Israel and Judah 1200 - 150 BC

READ	RESPOND	REFLECT	RECORD

When the queen of Sheba saw all the wisdom of Solomon
and the palace he had built, the food on his table,
the seating of his officials, the attending servants in
their robes, his cupbearers, and the burnt offerings
he made at the temple of the LORD,
she was overwhelmed.
1 Kings 10.4,5

BIBLE IN BRIEF

MONTH 2 WEEK 3
DIVIDED KINGDOMS 870 – 587 BC

Note: Israel,the northern kingdom, with 10 tribes , was much wealthier and more powerful than Judah. It was destroyed by Assyria in 722 BC, and Judah was brought to an end in 587 BC

Day 1   1 Kings 19 The prophet Elijah
How did Elijah come to hear God's voice?

Day 2   1 Kings 21 Royal greed and murder
What is your opinion of Ahab's character?

Day 3   2 Kings 5 Healing of an enemy general
A story of pride, humility, grace, greed and punishment. Who do you identify with most?

Day 4   2 Kings 9-10 A bloody coup 842 BC
Note: This turned all of Israel's former allies into enemies, and left it open to many invasions from Syria.
Is it ever right to kill in the name of religion?

Day 5   2 Kings 17.1-23 The end of Israel 721 BC
"They themselves became worthless" (v.15)
What are the marks of a decaying society?

Month 2: The History of Israel and Judah 1200 - 150 BC

READ RESPOND REFLECT RECORD

Elijah went before the people and said,
"How long will you waver between two opinions?
If the LORD is God, follow him,
but if Baal is God, follow him."
1 Kings 18.21

BIBLE IN BRIEF

Day 6　2 Kings 18+ 19.1-19, 35-end Hezekiah and the Assyrian threat 701 BC
How can we distinguish between faith and foolhardiness?

Day 7　2 Kings 23.1-23 Religious revival c. 620 BC
Note: The book of the law could be a version of Deuteronomy, brought south from Israel.
Are there idols in our personal lives or in our society that need to be dealt with?

Jehu submitting to the Assyrian king

Month 2: The History of Israel and Judah 1200 - 150 BC

READ	RESPOND	REFLECT	RECORD

The king stood by the pillar and
renewed the covenant in the presence
of the LORD – to follow the LORD,
and keep his commands, regulations and decrees
with all his heart and all his soul.
2 Kings 23.3

MONTH 2 WEEK 4
EXILE AND RESTORATION
587 – c. 167 BC

Day 1   2 Kings 25 Jerusalem destroyed by Babylon
Note: After several attempts to retain Judah as a client kingdom, Babylon finally destroyed it in 587 BC.
What hope remains after Jerusalem's fall?

Day 2   Haggai 1 Rebuilding the Temple 520 BC
Note: After conquering Babylon, the Persian king Cyrus allowed Jews to return to Judah in 537 BC.
Haggai calls for communal worship before private gain. Should we reset our priorities?

Day 3   Nehemiah 1-2 Rebuilding Jerusalem 446 BC
Note: A first-hand account, 100 years after the return.
What personal qualities made Nehemiah effective in the project to restore Jerusalem?

Day 4   Nehemiah 8 Ezra reads the Law to the people.
How did Ezra and the people express their love of God's Law?

Day 5   Daniel 1 Life in exile: keeping the food laws
Daniel and his friends made kosher food a priority. What might we treat as a priority to stay faithful to God in our secular society?

Month 2: The History of Israel and Judah 1200 - 150 BC

READ   **RESPOND**   **REFLECT**   **RECORD**

> It was because of the LORD's anger that all this happened to Jerusalem and Judah, and in the end he thrust them from his presence.
> 2 Kings 24.20

BIBLE IN BRIEF

Day 6   Daniel 6 Daniel and the Lion's Den
Note: A story reflecting the crisis in 168 BC when the Greek king of Persia tried to destroy Judaism.
How important is prayer in your life?

Day 7   Daniel 7 A vision of empires
Note: Daniel 7-12 are of visions of the end time – or of the political situation after Alexander the Great had conquered the Near East. The four beasts may represent four consecutive empires: Babylonian, Median, Persian & Greek.
How is the dominion of the "son of man" (vv.13-14) different from previous empires?

War captives being led into exile

Month 2: The History of Israel and Judah 1200 - 150 BC

READ	RESPOND	REFLECT	RECORD

"We will never find any basis for charges
against this man Daniel unless it has something to do
with the law of his God"
Daniel 6.5

THE OTHER SIDE
RIVAL EMPIRES

Only once is Israel mentioned in ancient Egyptian inscriptions. This comes from the victory monument of Pharaoh Merenptah (1223 – 1211), when Egypt was trying to keep Palestine within its sphere of influence, roughly around the period of the Judges.

> *The princes lie prostrate saying "Salaam".*
> *Not one lifts his head among the subject peoples*
> *(lit. Nine Bows).*
> *Destruction for Libya! Hatti is pacified.*
> *Canaan is plundered with every evil.*
> *Ashkelon is taken; Gaza is captured;*
> *Yanoam is made non-existent.*
> *Israel lies desolate, its seed is no more;*
> *Hurru has become a widow for Egypt.*
> *All the lands in their entirety are at peace.*
> *Everyone who was a nomad has been curbed by King Merenptah.*

In the 9th century BC Israel was a vassal to the Assyrian king. This comes from some bronze gates set up by the powerful king Shalmaneser III.

> *The tribute of Jehu son of Omri. I received from him silver, gold, a golden (unknown word) bowl, a golden vase with pointed bottom, golden tumblers, golden buckets, tin, a staff for the king and a wooden (unknown word).*

In 722 BC the new king of Assyria, Sargon II, captured Samaria and destroyed the northern kingdom of Israel.

Month 2: The History of Israel and Judah 1200 - 150 BC

At the beginning of my royal rule I besieged and conquered the town of the Samarians... I led away as prisoners 27,290 inhabitants and equipped from them soldiers to man 50 chariots for my royal corps... The town I rebuilt better than before and settled therein people from countries which I myself had conquered. I placed an officer of mine over them and imposed upon them tribute as is customary for Assyrian citizens.

In 701 Sargon's son Sennacherib captured many fortresses in Judah and besieged Jerusalem.

As to Hezekiah the Jew, he did not submit to my yoke. I laid siege to 46 of his strong cities, walled forts and countless small villages.... I drove out 200,150 people, young and old, male and female, horses, mules, donkeys, camels, big and small cattle beyond counting ... Himself I made a prisoner in Jerusalem, his royal residence, like a bird in a cage.... he did send me later, to Nineveh, my lordly city, together with 30 talents of gold, 800 talents of silver, precious stones, ... elephant hides, ebony wood, ... his daughters, concubines, male and female musicians.

A hundred years later, in 597 BC, the King of Babylon, Nebuchadnezzar II, besieged Jerusalem, took away the king Jehoiachin and installed the latter's uncle Zedekiah as king in his place. Later Zedekiah rebelled, and in 587 the Babylonians captured Jerusalem again, executed Zedekiah and destroyed the city and the temple. This refers to the first siege.
Note: Akkad means the country of the Babylonians.

BIBLE IN BRIEF

Year 7, month Kislumu: The king of Akkad moved his army into Hatti land, laid siege to the city of Judah and the king took the city of the second day of the month Addaru. He appointed in it a new king of his liking, took heavy booty from it and brought into Babylon.

The Babylonian empire collapsed when attacked by the Persian king Cyrus, and Babylon itself was taken without a fight. He then allowed the subject people, including the Jews, to return to their homeland and rebuild their sanctuaries. In the Bible, the unnamed prophet calls Cyrus the Messiah (meaning Anointed):

> "This is what the LORD says to his anointed,
> to Cyrus, whose right hand I have taken hold of,
> to subdue nations before him
> and to strip kings of their armour ..."
> (Isaiah 45.1-2)

And Cyrus did always endeavour to treat according to justice the black-headed Babylonians whom Marduk has made him conquer. Marduk, the great lord, protector of his people, beheld with pleasure Cyrus' good deeds and his upright heart. He ordered him to march against his city Babylon...

His widespread troops - their number, like that of a river, could not be established – strolled along, their weapons packed away. Without any battle, he made him enter his town of Babylon, sparing Babylon any calamity. He delivered into Cyrus' hands Nabonidus, the king who did not worship Marduk...

Month 2: The History of Israel and Judah 1200 - 150 BC

I am Cyrus, king of the world, legitimate king, king of Babylon, king of Sumer and Akkad … I returned to the sacred cities on the other side of the Tigris, the sanctuaries of which have been ruins for a long time, the images which used to live therein and established for them permanent sanctuaries. I also gathered all their former inhabitants and returned them to their habitations...

(translated by F.H.Weissbach and R.W.Rogers)

MONTH 3
THE PROPHETS

From 740 to 520 BC Israel and Judah were challenged by the towering prophetic figures of Isaiah, Jeremiah, Ezekiel and others.

Prophets had existed since the earliest times (like the company of prophets in 1 Samuel 10.5-6). Sometimes they wore coats of animal skin to show their reliance on the God who had led Israel during their desert wanderings under Moses. (2 Kings 1.8) Their function was to pronounce by words and actions the message that God wanted to give to the people. Unfortunately many of the official prophets simply spoke from their own wishful thinking. (Jeremiah 23.16-22).

In week 1 we meet the first prophets whose words were written and preserved – the so-called Writing Prophets – namely Amos, Hosea, Isaiah and Micah. They were called to be God's spokesmen around 740 BC, when Israel and Judah were apparently prosperous and secure.

They warned that God would bring disaster on the nation unless the people changed their ways, putting social justice first, and turning away from the worship of idols (which was basically a form of magic, trying to get the spirits to deliver what the devotees wanted). Their prophecies fell on deaf ears, certainly in Israel, the northern kingdom. Within 20 years, in 722 BC, the Assyrian empire destroyed Israel and took its whole population into exile.

A hundred years later, in 626 BC, Jeremiah, from a priestly family in the Judaean hills, was called to warn against the

Month 3: The Prophets

coming disaster, even though a godly king, Josiah, was then on the throne.

Jeremiah tried to shake the people out of their complacency and warned them that unless they turned back to God, their nation and Jerusalem would be destroyed as Israel and Samaria had been. He lived to see his words tragically fulfilled in the destruction of Jerusalem in 587 BC.

In week 3 we come to prophecies made in exile in Babylon. In the 590's the strange figure of Ezekiel appeared among the first wave of exiles in Babylon. He was a priest who had amazing visions, and who warned in words and strange symbolic actions against the facile optimism of the Jewish exiles. However, both Jeremiah and Ezekiel proclaimed the hope that after two generations God would bring his people back to their land.

About 540 BC an unnamed prophet announced that God was about to accomplish this miraculous restoration through the overthrow of Babylon by the Persian king Cyrus. Most scholars believe that this is the setting of Isaiah 40 - 55.

In week 4 we read the prophets who preached after Cyrus had allowed the subject peoples of Babylon to return to their ancestral lands.

The Jews were able to return to Jerusalem and rebuild the Temple. This however took longer and was harder than expected. The struggle to re-establish a godly people in Judaea was addressed in Isaiah 56-66, and in some of the shorter prophetic books at the end of the Old Testament.

BIBLE IN BRIEF

There are twelve short prophetic books, (referred to by the rabbis as "the Twelve"). They are not in any chronological order though the last three are probably the latest. The Twelve include the famous story of Jonah and the whale - actually a "great fish".

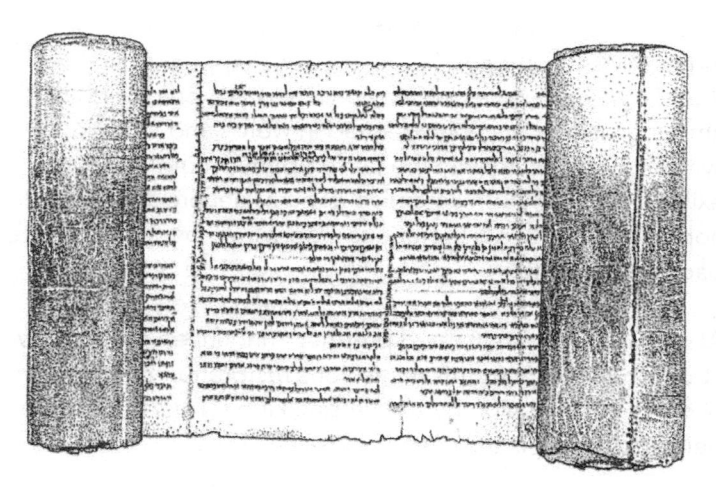

Isaiah scroll from the Dead Sea Scrolls

Month 3: The Prophets

Timeline of Prophets and Major Kings
(using Albright's calculations)

Judah	Prophets	Israel
House of David		*Civil war*
		House of Omri
Asa 913-873		Omri 876-869
		Founding of Samaria
Jehoshophat 873-849	Elijah	Ahab 869-850
	Elisha	+ son and grandson
Ahaziah 842		
Queen Athaliah 842-837		**House of Jehu**
Joash 837-800		Jehu 842-815
	Jonah	Jeroboam II 786-746
	Hosea	*Height of Israel's power*
	Amos	
Uzziah or Azariah		*Civil war*
783-742	Isaiah	**House of Menahem**
		Menahem 745-738
		+ son
		House of Pekah
Ahaz 735-715	Micah	Pekah 737-732
		House of Hoshea
Hezekiah 715-687		Hoshea 731-721
		Assyria destroys Israel 721
Nebuchadnezzer attacks Judah		
Manasseh 687-642		
Josiah 640-609	Zephaniah	
Religious reform	Jeremiah	
Jehoiakim 609-598		
(Jehoiachin)	Ezekiel	
Zedekiah 597-586		
Babylon destroys Judah 586		
	Isaiah 40-56	
Cyrus captures Babylon 540		

MONTH 3 WEEK 1
THE FALL OF ISRAEL 750-700 BC

Day 1   Amos 5 A farmer from Judah proclaims Israel's fall because the rich oppress the poor.
What actions does God hate?

Day 2   Hosea 4 A prophet from the northern kingdom of Israel proclaims judgement
Can we see examples of spiritual infidelity in our own lives and in our society?

Day 3   Micah 6 "What does the Lord require?"
How would following this change your life?

Day 4   Isaiah 6 God calls Isaiah to be his spokesman
Note: Place: the Temple, Jerusalem. Date: 742 BC
Notice the contrast between the vision of God's majesty in the Temple, and the task given to Isaiah. How might Isaiah feel about all this?

Day 5   Isaiah 1 The corruption of religion
What is wrong with religion which fails to include concern for social justice?

Month 3: The Prophets

READ **RESPOND** **REFLECT** **RECORD**

There is no faithfulness, no love,
no acknowledgement
of God in the land.
Hosea 4.1

Day 6   Isaiah 5 Judgement on social evil
When the rich get richer and the poor get poorer, what are the consequences, nationally and spiritually?

Day 7   Isaiah 11.1-9 Promise of a righteous king
How does this picture of God's ideal king compare with the current government? What is your hope?

Ivories from a palace in Samaria

Month 3: The Prophets

| READ | RESPOND | REFLECT | RECORD |

> Stop doing wrong, learn to do right!
> Seek justice, rebuke the oppressor.
> Defend the cause of the fatherless,
> plead the case of the widow.
> Isaiah 1.17

BIBLE IN BRIEF

MONTH 3 WEEK 2
THE FALL OF JUDAH c. 630–585 BC

Day 1   Jeremiah 1 God's call
God's call to Jeremiah involved walking a very lonely road. What road is God calling you to follow?

Day 2   Jeremiah 7 "Repent or perish"
What was wrong with the way the people of Judah lived?

Day 3   Jeremiah 26 Reactions to the message
Why was it so risky to be a God-fearing prophet? Do similar things happen today?

Day 4   Jeremiah 29 Message to the exiles
How can we tell the difference between the genuine promises of God and mere wish-fulfilment?

Day 5   Jeremiah 38 The king's last chance
King Zedekiah is portrayed not as evil but as weak and indecisive. How can we find the courage to make unpopular decisions?

Month 3: The Prophets

READ **RESPOND** **REFLECT** **RECORD**

This is the nation that has not
obeyed the LORD its God
or responded to correction.
Truth has perished;
it has vanished from their lips.
Jeremiah 7.28

BIBLE IN BRIEF

Day 6   Jeremiah 31.1-34 Promise of restoration
God says he is going to give Israel a fresh start.
Can you think of other occasions when God creates a new beginning?

Day 7   Lamentations 1 A lament over Jerusalem
Can faith and grief exist together?

"The tower of the old church is here to remember the judgment of God that broke upon our people in the war years"

From the plaque on the church tower destroyed by an air attack on Berlin, 23rd November 1943.

The Kaiser Wilhelm Memorial Church, Berlin

Month 3: The Prophets

| READ | RESPOND | REFLECT | RECORD |

This is the covenant that I will make
with the house of Israel after that time,
declares the LORD.
I will put my law in their minds
and write it on their hearts.
I will be their God, and they will be my people.
Jeremiah 31.33

MONTH 3 WEEK 3
SPEAKING FROM BABYLON c. 593-571 BC

Day 1   Ezekiel 1 + 2 A vision of God's glory
Draw or paint this account of "the appearance of the likeness of the glory of the Lord".

Day 2   Ezekiel 33 The prophet as watchman
Ezekiel is called to act faithfully whatever the outcome. How hard is it to do what we think is right and to leave the outcome to God?

Day 3   Ezekiel 37 Promise of restoration
Can these bones live?" Are there occasions when the apparently impossible happens?

SPEAKING FROM BABYLON c. 540 BC

Note: After Cyrus conquered Babylon in 540 BC, he allowed the captive peoples to return to their own countries.

Day 4   Isaiah 40 Good news is coming
The prophet's faith is that the God of creation is also the God of history. In this passage, where does he see God at work?

Day 5   Isaiah 42 The servant of the Lord
*God acts through his servant (the prophet? the people of Israel? someone to come?)
What is the character of the Lord's servant?*

Month 3: The Prophets

| READ | RESPOND | REFLECT | RECORD |

"You, my people, will know that I am the LORD,
when I open your graves and bring you up from them.
I will put my spirit in you and you will live."
Ezekiel 37.13,14

BIBLE IN BRIEF

Day 6   Isaiah 52.13-53 The suffering servant
Where do we best see this description of the suffering servant of the Lord fulfilled?

Day 7   Isaiah 55 An everlasting covenant
What is God offering to his people?

Ishtar Gate, Babylon

Month 3: The Prophets

READ   **RESPOND**   **REFLECT**   **RECORD**

"See, the former things have taken place,
and new things I declare;
before they spring into being,
I announce them to you."
Isaiah 42.9

MONTH 3 WEEK 4
HOPE AND DISAPOINTMENT
c. 540 – 460 BC

Day 1   Isaiah 58 The call to true religion c. 520 BC
Religion and social justice – natural allies or natural enemies?

Day 2   Isaiah 64 A prayer for help
The return to Jerusalem was a disappointment.
How can we pray in a situation of little apparent hope?

Day 3   Isaiah 25 A glorious vision for Jerusalem
Note: Isaiah 24-27 may be a later addition to the book of Isiah.
The vision of world-wide desolation seems pertinent today.
Are there any signs of hope?

Day 4   Jonah 1 + 2 Jonah and the great fish
Note: Jonah was a prophet in Israel around 750 BC. This book may be a sermon told as a story.
Nineveh, the capital of Assyria, fell in 612 BC.
Have you ever run (or walked) away from God?
With what consequences?

Month 3: The Prophets

READ	RESPOND	REFLECT	RECORD

Oh that you would rend the heavens and come down,
that the mountains would tremble before you!
Come down to make your name known
to your enemies and cause the nations
to quake before you!
Isaiah 64.1,2

BIBLE IN BRIEF

Day 5   Jonah 3 + 4 Jonah in Nineveh
Why was Jonah angry?
What aspects of Jonah's character are like you and what aspects are unlike?

Day 6   Zechariah 12 + 13 Triumph and repentance
Note: The writer and the date are unknown.
God says he will deal with external & internal threats. Can these sayings apply to life now?

Day 7 Malachi 3 + 4 God's coming judgement
The prophet longed to see a clear distinction between those who were good and those who were evil.
What do you feel about this?

A Persian Warrior

Month 3: The Prophets

| READ | RESPOND | REFLECT | RECORD |

Who can endure the day of his coming?
Malachi 3.2

THE OTHER SIDE
PRAYERS OF THE PEOPLES

Not strictly a prayer. This is a Hebrew child's writing exercise about 925 BC, the time of king Solomon, describing the agricultural year:

> *His two months are (olive) harvest,*
> *His two months are planting (grain),*
> *His two months are late planting;*
> *His month is hoeing up flax,*
> *His month is harvest of barley,*
> *His month is harvest and feasting;*
> *His two months are vine-tending,*
> *His month is summer fruit.*
> *(trans W.F. Albright)*

The religion of Baal was the great rival to the original religion of the Hebrews throughout the monarchy. Baal was a fertility god and/or the god of storms. A long epic poem about Baal was discovered in Ras Shamra in northern Syria around 1930. El is the supreme god, father of mankind and all living creatures, and was the one whom Abraham worshipped.

> "We came to the pleasance of Dabrland,
> to the beauty of Shihlmematfield.
> We came upon Baal
> fallen on the ground.
> Powerful Baal is dead,
> the Prince, Lord of the earth, is perished."
> Straightway Kindly El Benign
> descends from the throne,
> and sits on the ground;

> pours dust of mourning on his head,
>> earth of mortification on his pate...
> he cuts a gash with a stone …
>> he gashes his cheeks and his chin …
> He ploughs his chest like a garden
>> harrows his back like a plain.
> He lifts up his voice and cries,
> "Baal's dead! What becomes of the people?
>> Dagon's son – what of the masses? …

The result is a devastating drought.

Anath, Baal's sister then seeks out Mot, the god of death, who has killed Baal.

> Anath seizes the godly Mot,
>> with sword she doth cleave him …
>> with handmill she grinds him,
>> in the field she doth sow him …
>
> Behold, alive is Powerful Baal,
>> and behold, living is the Prince, Lord of Earth!
> In a dream, O Kindly El Benign,
> in a vision, Creator of creatures,
> The heavens rained down fat,
>> the wadis flowed with honey....
> So I knew that alive was powerful Baal,
>> living the Prince, Lord of the earth!

The complexities of ancient religion is brought out by the start of this vassal treaty of Esarhaddon, king of Assyria (681- 669 BC).

BIBLE IN BRIEF

> *The treaty of Esarhaddon, king of the world, king of Assyria, son of Sennacherib ...with Ramataya, city-ruler of Uraka- zabanu ...which he has made binding with you before Jupiter, Venus, Saturn, Mercury, Mars and Sirius; before Ashur, Anu, Enlil and Ea, Sin, Shamash, Adad and Marduk; Nabu, Nusku, Urash and Nergal; (the goddesses) Ninlil, Sherua and Belet-ili, Ishtar of Nineveh and Ishtar of Arbela; all the gods dwelling in heaven and earth, the gods of Assyria, the gods of Sumer and Akkad, the gods of every foreign country....*

A Sumerian prayer from the library of Ashurbanipal (668-633 BC) addressed to all the gods.

> *May the fury of my lord's heart be quieted toward me.*
> *May the god who is not known be quieted toward me.*
> *May the goddess who is not known be quieted toward me...*
> *O god whom I know or do not know,*
> *my transgressions are many, great are my sins.*
> *O goddess whom I know or do not know,*
> *my transgressions are many, great are my sins.*
> *The transgressions which I have committed,*
> *indeed I do not know.*
> *The sin which I have done, indeed I do not know....*
> *The god in the rage of his heart confronted me.*
> *The goddess was angry, she made me become ill....*
> *I utter laments, but no one hears me.*
> *I am troubled; I am overwhelmed; I cannot see.*
> *O my god, merciful one, I address to thee the prayer, "Ever incline to me."*
> *I kiss the feet of the goddess; I crawl before thee...*

Month 3: The Prophets

A prayer of Nebuchadnezzar II (634-562 BC) to Marduk, god of Babylon.

> *O Marduk, my lord, do remember my deeds favourably as good, may my good deeds be always before your mind, so that my walking in Esagila* and Ezida** – which I love – may last to old age.*
>
> *May I remain always your legitimate governor, may I pull your yoke till I am sated with progeny, may my name be remembered in future days in a good sense, may my offspring rule forever over the black-headed***.*

* Esagila was a large temple complex in Babylon dedicated to Marduk

** Ezida was a temple in Borsippa dedicated to Nabu, the god of wisdom and learning

*** The black-headed were the inhabitants of Sumer, the earliest civilisation of Mesopotamia, modern Iraq.

Nergal, Babylonian god of war and death

MONTH 4
LAW, PSALMS AND WISDOM

The word "Bible" comes from the Greek "Biblia", which means "Books" - plural. It is a reminder that the Bible is actually a library of 66 named books. The major division is between the Old Testament, written in Hebrew, and the New Testament, written in Greek – the common language of the Roman Empire.

Of course, Jews don't refer to their scriptures as "Old" nor did Jesus. The phrase he used was "the Law and the Prophets". This is still part of the modern Jewish expression, "Tanakh", which incorporates the three major aspects:

T = Torah – meaning Teaching or Law: the first five books from Genesis to Deuteronomy.
N = Nevi'im – meaning prophets, including the histories: Joshua, Judges, 1 & 2 Samuel, 1 & 2 Kings etc.
K = K'tuvim - meaning Writings, which record practical wisdom for daily life, worship songs (psalms) well as religious debate.

In month 1 we sampled the stories of the founding fathers of Judaism as set out in the Torah. But we did not touch on the law and regulations which formed the framework for community life. We look at these in week 1.
Note: Deuteronomy probably came from the northern kingdom of Israel in the 8th century.

In weeks 2 and 3 we read 10 of the 150 psalms. The Psalms were the hymn book of ancient Israel, and are still central to the worship of Jews and Christians.

Month 4: Law, Psalms and Wisdom

Jesus quoted them twice on the cross. The psalms cover the whole range of human emotion, from despair to joy, from complaint to thanksgiving, from doubt to faith. There are personal prayers, national laments, songs reflecting Israel's history. My hope is that reading these 10 psalms will encourage us to discover some of their riches for ourselves, and to use them in our own prayers.

Books were written all over the ancient Middle East to give guidance in how to live prosperous and moral lives, and to grapple with the problem of suffering. Weeks 3 and 4 introduce us to Proverbs, Job and Ecclesiastes. They face unflinchingly some of the most difficult questions of life and give, not a facile answer, but an approach which involves honest grappling with the big questions.

Several books were written in the 200 years before Christ. They were written in Greek and by 100 AD had been pushed aside by the synagogue but embraced by the church. They are called "the Apocrypha", meaning hidden writings. They include books of history, moral fables, and religious teachings. In the 16th century, Martin Luther, the Protestant reformer, separated them from the standard Bible, so most Bibles in protestant countries do not have them, though Roman Catholic Bibles do. They are not included in this selection, but are easy to get hold of, and some passages are quoted in the section that follows, "The In Between".

MONTH 4 WEEK 1
THE LAW

Day 1 Leviticus 16 The Day of Atonement
In all the ancient world, animal sacrifice was the main way of worship. What might the details of the Day of Atonement symbolise?

Day 2 Leviticus 19 "Be holy" - rules for living
Draw three columns - Agree / Disagree / Not Sure. Put each of the commands under one of the columns. Which are the most interesting?

Day 3 Leviticus 25.1-43 Jubilee - a debt-free society
"The land is mine." (v.23) What is the basis of this policy of putting social equality before a free market? What might be the results?

Day 4 Judges 17 & 18 A disgraceful story
This story shows the kind of behaviour that the Law tried to eradicate. What might Micah and the Danites say to justify their conduct?

Day 5 Deuteronomy 6 "The Lord our God is one"
Note: The "Shema'a", "Hear, O Israel, the Lord our God, the Lord is the one..." v.4-9, and was used by Jesus and is used at all Jewish daily prayers.
Why should we obey God's commandments?

Month 4: Law, Psalms and Wisdom

READ   **RESPOND**   **REFLECT**   **RECORD**

Love the LORD your God with all your heart
and with all your soul and with all your strength.
Love your neighbour as yourself.
Deuteronomy 6.5, Leviticus 19.18

BIBLE IN BRIEF

Day 6   Deuteronomy 16 The three major festivals
"You shall keep the festival at the place that the Lord your God will choose." (v.15) What is the benefit of the whole community gathering together regularly for worship and celebration?

Day 7   Deuteronomy 30 "Choose life!"
Is God's love conditional? Or do we always have the possibility of "choosing life"?

Blowing the ram's horn or shofar

Month 4: Law, Psalms and Wisdom

READ	RESPOND	REFLECT	RECORD

> "This day I call heaven and earth
> as witnesses against you
> that I have set before you life and death,
> blessings and curses.
> Now choose life."
> Deuteronomy 30.19

MONTH 4 WEEK 2
DEVOTIONAL PSALMS

The Psalms are the prayer book of the Bible and were used by Jesus. They are the foundation of Jewish worship, and have been the ground of Christian prayer for 2,000 years.

The following are seven psalms that can be used in our own personal devotions. As you read them, choose one verse in each which means something to you and write it out.

Day 1   Psalm 51   "Have mercy on me"
Note: The Syrian Orthodox Church prays psalms 51, 63 and 113 every morning).
Day 2   Psalm 86   "Teach me your way"
Day 3   Psalm 27   "The Lord is my light"
Day 4   Psalm 103   "Bless the Lord, O my soul"
Day 5   Psalm 91   Traditional psalm for night time
Day 6   Psalm 139   "Where can I go from your Spirit?"
Day 7   Psalm 96   "Sing to the Lord a new song"

Egyptian Musicians

Month 4: Law, Psalms and Wisdom

READ **RESPOND** **REFLECT** **RECORD**

MONTH 4 WEEK 3
PSALMS AND SAYINGS

Day 1   Psalm 119.1-16 "I delight in your decrees"
Note: The lines of each group of 8 verses start with a different Hebrew letter: 1-8: Aleph; 9-16: Beth etc.
What are the results of "walking according to the law of the Lord"?

Day 2   Psalm 73 Why do the wicked prosper?
Do you know any examples where "the arrogant" and "the wicked" come to ruin?

Day 3   Psalm 148 Praise of God in creation
What does "all things praising God" mean?

Day 4   Psalm 105 Praise of God in Israel's history
What was the purpose and end result of God's championing of Israel?

(Compare with Psalm 106 for a rather more pessimistic account).

Day 5   Proverbs 2 A guide for life
In two columns write what makes up the character of the upright, and the character of the wicked.
Are there lessons for us in this?

Month 4: Law, Psalms and Wisdom

READ   **RESPOND**   **REFLECT**   **RECORD**

The LORD is my light and my salvation
- whom shall I fear?
Psalm 27.1

Day 6   Proverbs 8 Wisdom at creation
Wisdom is the aspect of God that teaches us to live well. What is her character?

Day 7   Proverbs 22 Sayings of the wise
Note: vv. 17-29 were taken from the Egyptian book "Instruction of Amen-em-opet"
Out of the 20 separate sayings in this chapter, what are your three favourites?

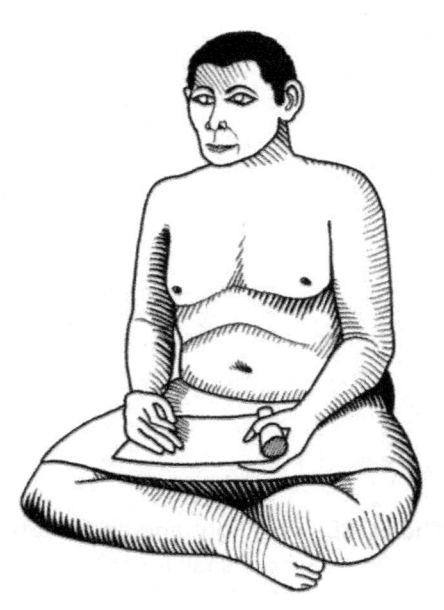

Egyptian Scribe

Month 4: Law, Psalms and Wisdom

READ **RESPOND** **REFLECT** **RECORD**

The fear of the Lord is the beginning of wisdom
Psalm 111.10

MONTH 4 WEEK 4
SUFFERING AND FUTILITY

Day 1   Job 1-2 Disaster strikes a righteous man
"Shall we accept good from God and not trouble?" Think of someone you know whose life has fallen apart. How did they react?

Day 2   Job 3 Job curses the day of his birth
What might it be like to feel that death is preferable to life?

Day 3   Job 15 A friend replies
What is wrong with Eliphaz's speech?

Day 4   Job 19 "The hand of God has struck me"
What are the causes of Job's despair – and where does the glimmer of hope come from?

Day 5   Job 38, 42 The Lord answers Job
God does not answer Job directly, but challenges him to change his perspective – to look at the wonder of the universe. How does this change things for Job?

Month 4: Law, Psalms and Wisdom

READ	RESPOND	REFLECT	RECORD

> Have pity on me, my friends,
> have pity, For the hand of God
> has struck me.
> Job 19:21

BIBLE IN BRIEF

Day 6   Ecclesiastes 1, 3 Life is meaningless
If death is the end, is stoical acceptance the best that can be offered? What can give our life meaning?

Day 7   Song of Songs 2 A love song
This poem of romantic passion has often been taken as a parable of spiritual passion. Where in your life are you passionate?

Catacombs in Jerusalem

Month 4: Law, Psalms and Wisdom

READ	RESPOND	REFLECT	RECORD

Here is the conclusion of the matter:
Fear God and obey his commandments,
For this is the whole duty of man.
Ecclesiastes 12:13

THE IN BETWEEN

The last writings of the Hebrew Old Testament probably date from around 400 BC, with the possible exception of Daniel. Because the majority of Jews now lived outside Palestine and spoke Greek, the Old Testament was translated into Greek and called the Septuagint (meaning 70, because it was believed that 70 scholars had translated it). Many books were written in Greek and formed an integral part of the Christian church's Bible until Martin Luther separated them out into a special section between the two Testaments in 1534. They then formed the Apocrypha (hidden things), and all the following writings come from these books.

The problems of translation
What was originally expressed in Hebrew does not have exactly the same sense when translated into another language. Not only this book, but even the Law itself, the Prophecies, and the rest of the books differ not a little when read in the original. (from Ecclesiasticus, Prologue)

In 167 BC there was the great revolt of Jews led by the Maccabee brothers which astonishingly succeeded in defeating the enormous Seleucid empire – the Persian empire which had been handed over to one of Alexander the Great's Greek generals.

History 330 – 179 BC
After Alexander son of Philip, the Macedonian, who came from the land of Kittim, had defeated King Darius of the Persians and the Medes, he succeeded him as king. (He had previously become king of Greece.) He fought many battles, conquered strongholds, and put to death the kings of the earth.

He advanced to the ends of the earth, and plundered many nations. When the earth became quiet before him, he was exalted, and his heart was lifted up. He gathered a very strong army and ruled over countries, nations, and princes, and they became tributary to him.

After this he fell sick and perceived that he was dying. So he summoned his most honoured officers, who had been brought up with him from youth, and divided his kingdom among them while he was still alive. And after Alexander had reigned for twelve years, he died.

Then his officers began to rule, each in his own place. They all put on crowns after his death, and so did their descendants after them for many years; and they caused many evils on the earth.

From them came forth a sinful root, Antiochus Epiphanes, son of King Antiochus; he had been a hostage in Rome. He began to reign in the one hundred and thirty-seventh year of the kingdom of the Greeks (175 BC).

Conflict within Israel
In those days certain renegades came out from Israel and misled many, saying, 'Let us go and make a covenant with the Gentiles around us, for since we separated from them many disasters have come upon us.' This proposal pleased them, and some of the people eagerly went to the king, who authorised them to observe the ordinances of the Gentiles. So they built a gymnasium in Jerusalem, according to Gentile custom, and removed the marks of circumcision, and abandoned the holy covenant. They joined with the Gentiles and sold themselves to do evil. (1 Maccabees 1.1-15)

Antiochus sides with the modernisers
Then the king wrote to his whole kingdom that all should be one people, and that all should give up their particular customs. All the Gentiles accepted the command of the king. Many even from Israel gladly adopted his religion; they sacrificed to idols and profaned the sabbath. And the king sent letters by messengers to Jerusalem and the towns of Judah; he directed them to follow customs strange to the land, to forbid burnt-offerings and sacrifices and drink - offerings in the sanctuary, to profane sabbaths and festivals, to defile the sanctuary and the priests, to build altars and sacred precincts and shrines for idols, to sacrifice swine and other unclean animals, and to leave their sons uncircumcised. They were to make themselves abominable by everything unclean and profane, so that they would forget the law and change all the ordinances. He added, 'And whoever does not obey the command of the king shall die.' (1 Maccabees 1.41-50)

Start of the revolt
Then the king's officers spoke to Mattathias as follows: 'You are a leader, honoured and great in this town, and supported by sons and brothers. Now be the first to come and do what the king commands, as all the Gentiles and the people of Judah and those that are left in Jerusalem have done. Then you and your sons will be numbered among the Friends of the king, and you and your sons will be honoured with silver and gold and many gifts.'

But Mattathias answered and said in a loud voice: 'Even if all the nations that live under the rule of the king obey him, and have chosen to obey his commandments, everyone of them abandoning the religion of their ancestors, I and my sons and my brothers will continue to live by the covenant of our ancestors. Far be it from us to desert the law and the ordinances. We will not obey the king's words by turning aside from our religion to the right hand or to the left.'

When he had finished speaking these words, a Jew came forward in the sight of all to offer sacrifice on the altar in Modein, according to the king's command.

When Mattathias saw it, he burned with zeal and his heart was stirred. He gave vent to righteous anger; he ran and killed him on the altar. At the same time he killed the king's officer who was forcing them to sacrifice, and he tore down the altar. Thus he burned with zeal for the law, just as Phinehas did against Zimri son of Salu. (see Numbers 25.7-8)

Then Mattathias cried out in the town with a loud voice, saying: 'Let everyone who is zealous for the law and supports the covenant come out with me!' Then he and his sons fled to the hills and left all that they had in the town. At that time many who were seeking righteousness and justice went down to the wilderness to live there, they, their sons, their wives, and their livestock, because troubles pressed heavily upon them. (1 Maccabees 2.17-30)

Judas Maccabaeus takes command

Then his son Judas, who was called Maccabeus, took command in his father's place. He was like a lion in his deeds, like a lion's cub roaring for prey. He searched out and pursued those who broke the law; he burned those who troubled his people.

Apollonius now gathered together Gentiles and a large force from Samaria to fight against Israel. When Judas learned of it, he went out to meet him, and he defeated and killed him. Many were wounded and fell, and the rest fled. Then they seized their spoils; and Judas took the sword of Apollonius, and used it in battle for the rest of his life. (1 Maccabees 3.1, 4-5, 10-12)

There followed many battles, most of which the Maccabees won – there are another 13 chapters of battles and politics.

The temple worship is re-established
Then Judas and his brothers said, 'See, our enemies are crushed; let us go up to cleanse the sanctuary and dedicate it.' So all the army assembled and went up to Mount Zion. There they saw the sanctuary desolate, the altar profaned, and the gates burned. In the courts they saw bushes sprung up as in a thicket, or as on one of the mountains. They saw also the chambers of the priests in ruins. Then they tore their clothes and mourned with great lamentation; they sprinkled themselves with ashes and fell face down on the ground. And when the signal was given with the trumpets, they cried out to Heaven.

Then Judas detailed men to fight against those in the citadel until he had cleansed the sanctuary. He chose blameless priests devoted to the law, and they cleansed the sanctuary and removed the defiled stones to an unclean place. They deliberated what to do about the altar of burnt-offering, which had been profaned. And they thought it best to tear it down, so that it would not be a lasting shame to them that the Gentiles had defiled it. So they tore down the altar, and stored the stones in a convenient place on the temple hill until a prophet should come to tell what to do with them. Then they took unhewn stones, as the law directs, and built a new altar like the former one. They also rebuilt the sanctuary and the interior of the temple, and consecrated the courts. They made new holy vessels, and brought the lampstand, the altar of incense, and the table into the temple. Then they offered incense on the altar and lit the lamps on the lampstand, and these gave light in the temple. They placed the bread on the table and hung up the curtains. Thus they finished all the work they had undertaken.

So they rose and offered sacrifice, as the law directs, on the new altar of burnt-offering that they had built. At the very season and on the very day that the Gentiles had profaned it, it was dedicated with songs and harps and lutes and cymbals. All the people fell on their faces and worshipped and blessed Heaven, who had prospered them. They celebrated the dedication of the altar for eight days, and joyfully offered burnt-offerings. There was very great joy among the people, and the disgrace brought by the Gentiles was removed.
(1 Maccabees 4.36-58, edited)

Note: This is celebrated by Jews today in the festival of Hanukkah in December.

Jonathan is appointed high priest
In the one hundred and sixtieth year (159 BC) Alexander Epiphanes, son of Antiochus, landed and occupied Ptolemais. Now King Alexander heard of the battles that Jonathan and his brothers had fought, of the brave deeds that they had done, and of the troubles that they had endured. So he said, 'Shall we find another such man? Come now, we will make him our friend and ally.'

And he wrote a letter and sent it to him, in the following words: 'King Alexander to his brother Jonathan, greetings. We have heard about you, that you are a mighty warrior and worthy to be our friend. And so we have appointed you today to be the high priest of your nation; you are to be called the king's Friend and you are to take our side and keep friendship with us.' He also sent him a purple robe and a golden crown.

So Jonathan put on the sacred vestments at the festival of booths, and he recruited troops and equipped them with arms in abundance. (1 Maccabees 10.1, 15-21 edited)

New theologies

The experience of the Maccabean revolt challenged Jewish believers as to the fate of those who died, often after torture, in order to stay true to the Law and their God. There came for many a strengthened belief in the reward of eternal life for the faithful. This was opposed by more conservative Jews.
This dispute is clearly set out in the Wisdom of Solomon, a book written in Alexandria shortly before the birth of Jesus.

The temple of Solomon

They reasoned unsoundly, saying to themselves,
'Short and sorrowful is our life....
and no one has been known to return from Hades.
For we were born by mere chance,
and hereafter we shall be as though we had never been,
for the breath in our nostrils is smoke,
and reason is a spark kindled by the beating of our hearts;
when it is extinguished, the body will turn to ashes,
and the spirit will dissolve like empty air...

'Let us lie in wait for the righteous man,
because he is inconvenient to us
and opposes our actions...
We are considered by him as something base,
and he avoids our ways as unclean;
he calls the last end of the righteous happy
and boasts that God is his father.
Let us see if his words are true,
and let us test what will happen at the end of his life...
Let us test him with insult and torture,
so that we may find out how gentle he is...
Let us condemn him to a shameful death,
for, according to what he says, he will be protected.'

Thus they reasoned, but they were led astray,
for their wickedness blinded them,
and they did not know the secret purposes of God,
nor hoped for the wages of holiness;
for God created us for incorruption,
and made us in the image of his own eternity,
but through the devil's envy death entered the world,
and those who belong to his company experience it.

But the souls of the righteous are in the hand of God,
and no torment will ever touch them.
In the eyes of the foolish they seemed to have died,
and their departure was thought to be a disaster,
and their going from us to be their destruction;
but they are at peace.

For though in the sight of others they were punished,
their hope is full of immortality.
Like gold in the furnace God tried them,
and like a sacrificial burnt-offering he accepted them.
In the time of their visitation they will shine forth,
and will run like sparks through the stubble.
They will govern nations and rule over peoples,
and the Lord will reign over them for ever.

(Wisdom of Solomon 2.1-4, 12-24, 3.1-8 edited)

Around 64 AD an educated Jewish Christian teacher wrote what we know as the Letter to the Hebrews. There is a short passage in it which shows how the Maccabean struggle was remembered two hundred years later:

And what more should I say? For time would fail me to tell of Gideon, Barak, Samson, Jephthah, of David and Samuel and the prophets - who through faith conquered kingdoms, administered justice, obtained promises, shut the mouths of lions, quenched raging fire, escaped the edge of the sword, won strength out of weakness, became mighty in war, put foreign armies to flight. Women received their dead by resurrection. Others were tortured, refusing to accept release, in order to obtain a better resurrection. Others suffered mocking and flogging, and even chains and imprisonment.

They were stoned to death, they were sawn in two, they were killed by the sword; they went about in skins of sheep and goats, destitute, persecuted, tormented - of whom the world was not worthy. They wandered in deserts and mountains, and in caves and holes in the ground.

Yet all these, though they were commended for their faith, did not receive what was promised, since God had provided something better so that they would not, without us, be made perfect. (Hebrews 11.32-40)

MONTH 5
JESUS

Here we come to more familiar territory. Many know of the four gospels, Matthew, Mark, Luke and John. These are the source of virtually all we know about Jesus. The word "Gospel" is the Anglo-Saxon translation of the Greek "Evangellion", both meaning Good News.

The first three weeks cover Jesus' ministry and death as recorded in Matthew, Mark and Luke. They share a lot of common material; indeed most scholars accept that both Luke and Matthew used Mark as a source, as well as having their own sources.

I am convinced that Mark is the earliest gospel, written about 50 AD, within 20 years of Jesus crucifixion, by someone who was present with Jesus in Gethsemane. (Mark 14: 51, 52)

Luke, a Greek doctor, wrote two books, his Gospel, which has some of Jesus' most famous parables, and the Acts of the Apostles. The latter ends with Paul under house arrest in Rome, about 62 AD. It is my belief that Luke wrote his Gospel and the Acts in 58 - 62 AD, with Mark as one of his sources. Matthew's Gospel was probably compiled some years later.

John is completely different. It was known early on as "the spiritual gospel". Some passages read like a meditation on the words of Jesus. But all his place references reflect Palestine before the Jewish War of 68 AD. The earliest fragment of the New Testament has verses from John's Gospel. It was written about 125 AD and is kept in the Ryland's library in Manchester.

Month 5: Jesus

This means that all we are told about Jesus was written in the first century, within the lifetime of many of his disciples.

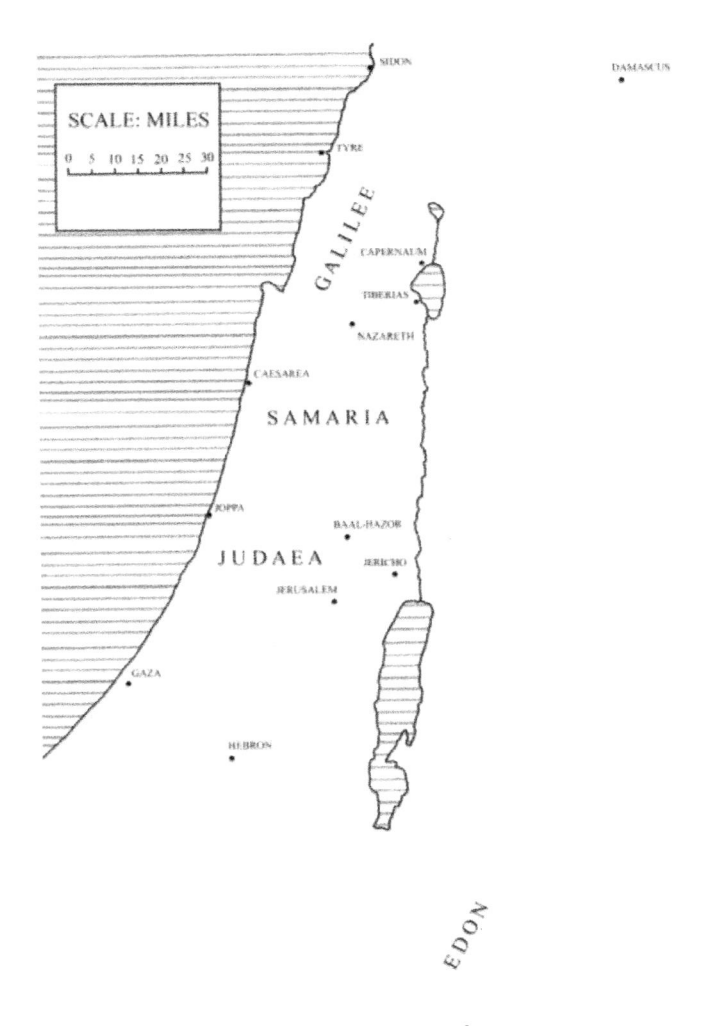

Palestine at the time of Jesus

MONTH 5 WEEK 1
STARTING UP & TEACHING

Day 1   Luke 2.1-21 Birth in Bethlehem

Note 1: Joseph may have come north to Nazareth to work as a carpenter/builder in the new city of Sepphoris 5 miles from Nazareth. How else might he have met Mary?

Note 2: The word "inn" actually means "guest room" as in the story of the last supper in Luke 22.11, i.e. a dining room in a large family house. The most private place for Mary would have been the basement cave used normally for the animals.

Note 3: "Jesus" is the Greek version of the Hebrew "Yeshua" or "Joshua". It means "God saves" - see Matthew 1.21.

Note 4: "Christ" is the Greek for the Hebrew "Messiah" or "Anointed". In the Hebrew scriptures the king and the high priest were anointed as God's representatives to rule and to lead worship (see Psalm 133 v.2) - "the Messiah of David" and "the Messiah of Aaron" are mentioned in the the Dead Sea scrolls. Some Jews hoped for one person to come as God's final representative.

What a contrast between the humble circumstances of Jesus' birth and the supernatural events that accompanied it.
If you were one of the shepherds, what would you think was going on?

Month 5: Jesus

READ **RESPOND** **REFLECT** **RECORD**

The virgin will be with child and
will give birth to a son,
and they will call him "Immanuel"
which means, "God with us."
Matthew 1.23 / Isaiah 7.14

Day 2   Mark 1.1-20 Baptism & the first followers
The beginning of Mark's gospel is written almost in "telegraphese". What would you like more information about
- *John the Baptist's preaching,*
- *or Jesus' time in the wilderness,*
- *or Jesus' preaching,*
- *or previous encounters between Jesus and his first disciples?*

Day 3   Mark 2.1-17 Healing & controversy
"I have not come to call the righteous, but sinners."
What do you think of Jesus' proclamation of forgiveness?

Day 4   Mark 4.1-20 Four responses to God's word
What kind of soil (or soils) are you?

Day 5   Matthew 5.1-16 True happiness
Note: The word Beatitude comes from the Latin word for Blessed or Happy (pronounced 'be-attitude')
The first few are mirrored in Luke 6:20-22
Jesus' Beatitudes are counter-intuitive to say the least. Can you make sense of them?

Bethlehem around 1950

Month 5: Jesus

READ **RESPOND** **REFLECT** **RECORD**

The crowds were amazed at Jesus' teaching,
Because he taught as one who had authority
Matthew 7 28:29

BIBLE IN BRIEF

Day 6 Matthew 5.21-48 The new law
Are Jesus' demands impossibly high? Or are they goals at which to aim, a life-long journey? Or can Jesus change me so I am able to walk his way? Did Jesus live like that?

Day 7 Matthew 6.19-34 God & money
Is Jesus' teaching about money good news or bad news? Or does it act like a lighthouse, showing our position, where we actually are?

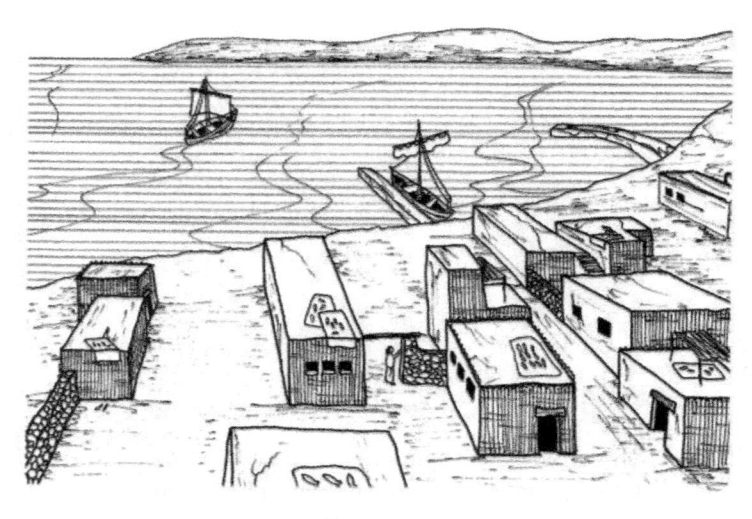

Capernaum

Month 5: Jesus

READ	RESPOND	REFLECT	RECORD

"The pagan world runs after all such things,
and your Father knows you need them.
But seek his kingdom, and these things will
be given to you as well."
Luke 12: 30-31

MONTH 5 WEEK 2
THE MISSION INTENSIFIES

Day 1   Mark 5.21-43 Two healings
Notice Jesus' mastery over life and healing; and his focus on the person in front of him. Imagine the scene and put yourself in the story. Who would you be? What might Jesus be saying to you?

Day 2   Mark 8.27 – 9.13 'Who do you say that I am?'
Who is Jesus? What is his calling – and our calling?

Day 3   Luke 10.1-24 Sending the disciples out
What did Jesus send his disciples out to do? What does he say about himself?

Day 4   Luke 10.25-42 The good Samaritan
Notice that Jesus does not answer the scribe's question. What does he do instead?
+
What is his attitude to busyness and stillness?

Month 5: Jesus

READ **RESPOND** **REFLECT** **RECORD**

A voice came from the cloud,
"This is my Son, whom I love. Listen to him."
Mark 9:7

Day 5   Luke 11.1-13 Teaching on prayer
Think through each line of this short version of the Lord's Prayer and how it reflects Jesus' teaching.
What does Jesus promise if we pray?

Day 6   Luke 15 A lost coin and a lost son
The heart of the gospel. Does the elder brother have an argument, or has he missed the point?

Day 7   Mark 11.1-19 Entry into Jerusalem
Jesus entered Jerusalem as publicly as he could, and then occupied the large outer court of the Temple, the Court of the Gentiles. Why?

Note: At Passover the population of Jerusalem trebled to 150,000, including thousands of Galilean pilgrims wanting to support "their" prophet. The Jerusalem authorities were furious but powerless - for now.

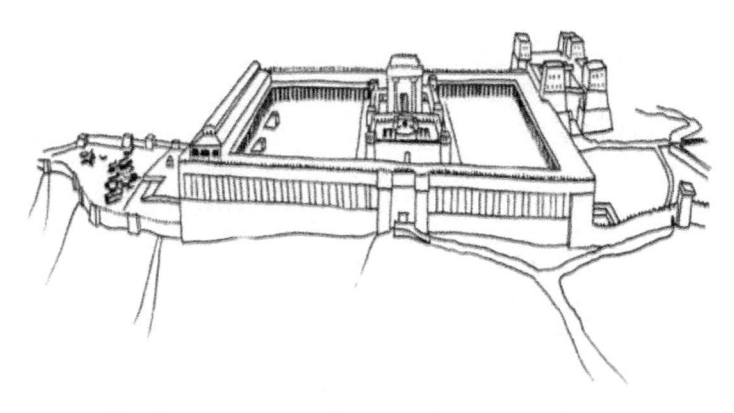

The Temple in Jerusalem and the Antonia fortress

Month 5: Jesus

READ **RESPOND** **REFLECT** **RECORD**

"There will be more rejoicing in heaven
over one sinner who repents
than over ninety-nine righteous persons
who do not need to repent."
Luke 15:7

MONTH 5 WEEK 3
THE FINAL CHALLENGE

Day 1 Mark 12.1-34 Confrontation.
How does Jesus counter the challenges of his opponents? What can we learn from his replies?
Note: "Hear, O Israel.." is the "Shema'a ", the ABC of the Jewish faith. (Deuteronomy 6.4),

Day 2 Mark 14.12-26 The last supper
Note: The disciples assumed that the betrayal of Jesus to the authorities would be unintentional.
What was Jesus trying to communicate when he said, "This is my body", "This is my blood"?

Day 3 Mark 14.27-50 Agony in Gethsemane
At his lowest, Jesus prayed, "Not my will but yours be done." Can you pray the same way?
Note: The young man in v. 51-52 was probably Mark, the writer of the gospel.

Day 4 Mark 14.52-15.15 Jesus on trial
What charges were brought against Jesus?
What were the chief priests, Peter, Pilate and the crowd actually afraid of?
Note: The crowd were almost certainly from Jerusalem, not the Galilean pilgrims of Palm Sunday, Mark 11.

Month 5: Jesus

READ	RESPOND	REFLECT	RECORD

"Abba, Father, everything is possible for you.
Take this cup from me.
Yet not what I will, but what you will."
Mark 14.36

Day 5   Mark 15.16-47 The crucifixion
"My God, my God, why have you forsaken me?" (Psalm 22.1) Did Jesus mean physical pain, mental agony or spiritual desolation?
Note: Is there a clue in Galatians 3.13, "Christ ...became a curse for us, as it is written, 'Cursed is everyone who hangs on a tree'" (Deuteronomy 21.23)

Day 6   Mark 16.1-8 Resurrection?
The story breaks off virtually mid-sentence, equivalent of a series of dots. What clues are there as to what happened before and after?

Day 7   Luke 24.13-35 Resurrection!
When the disciples met Jesus risen from death, how might their world view have changed?

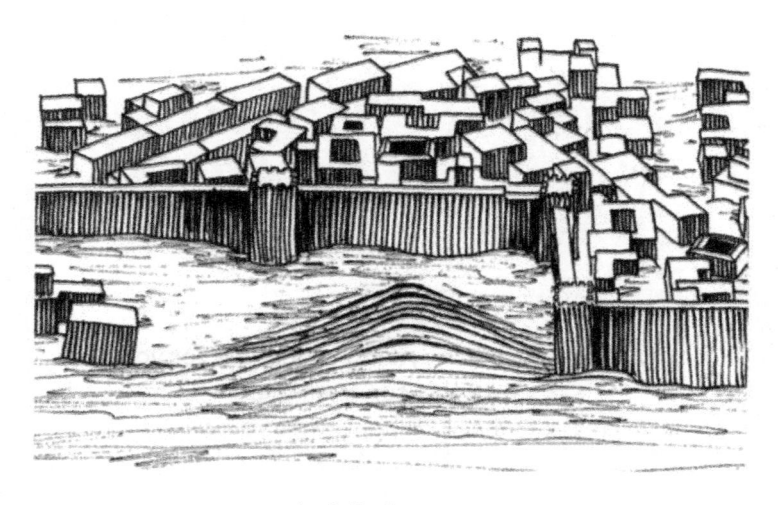

The hill of Golgotha

Month 5: Jesus

READ   **RESPOND**   **REFLECT**   **RECORD**

> He poured out his life unto death
> and was numbered with
> the transgressors.
> Isaiah 53.12

BIBLE IN BRIEF

MONTH 5 WEEK 4
THE GOSPEL OF JOHN

Day 1   John 1.1-18 The Eternal Word
A proclamation that in Jesus we see the full character of God - "the image of the invisible God" (Colossians 1.15) List the words John uses to describe him.

Day 2   John 3.1-21 Born of the Spirit
Note: When the New Testament was written, there were no punctuation marks and no lower case letters. The words of Jesus could end at verse 12 or 15 or 21, the rest being John's commentary. What do you think?
What might "Being born of water and spirit (or Spirit) mean?

Day 3   John 6.1-59 Feeding of 5,000 & the true bread
What does the miracle of the multiplication of the loaves mean?
Note: This is the only miracle reported in all four gospels. Compare it to the story of the manna in the desert (Exodus 16).

Day 4   John 11.1-53 Jesus raises a friend from death
What does Jesus mean when he says, "I am the resurrection and the life"?

Day 5   John 14 The Father, the Son & the Spirit
What relations are there between the Father, the Son and the Spirit? Try to draw a diagram!

Month 5: Jesus

READ **RESPOND** **REFLECT** **RECORD**

"I am the living bread that came down from heaven."
John 6.51

BIBLE IN BRIEF

Day 6   John 18.28 – 19.30 The trial under Pilate
What did the title "King of the Jews" mean to the chief priests, Pilate, the crowd, the soldiers and to Jesus? What did Jesus mean when he said, "It is finished"?

Day 7   John 20 Resurrection!
Make a list of the events of that first day of the week. Why might it be easier for us to believe than for Thomas?

Palestinian women grinding coffee

Month 5: Jesus

READ **RESPOND** **REFLECT** **RECORD**

This is eternal life:
that they may know you, the only true God,
and Jesus Christ, whom you have sent.
John 17.3

THE OTHER SIDE

Jesus did not teach and heal in a vacuum. The Jewish Palestine of his day was a hotbed of religious and political dispute, some of which is reflected in the gospels. We have evidence for this in the writings of Josephus, a Jew born in 37AD who witnessed the siege and destruction of Jerusalem in 70 AD and subsequently wrote about it. His quotations come from "The Jewish War", written in 75 AD, Penguin Classics. We also have many of the surviving traditions quoted in a brilliant little book on the life of Yohanan ben Zakkai, a crucial figure in the rebirth of Judaism after the fall of the Temple, by the Jewish historian Jacob Neusner, published 1962. All quotes apart from those of Josephus are taken from Neusner's book, apart from two from "Jesus the Jew" by G. Vermes.

Among the Jews there are three schools of thought, whose adherents are called Pharisees, Sadducees and Essenes respectively.... Of the two schools named first, the Pharisees are held to be the most authoritative exponents of the Law and count as the leading sect. They ascribe everything to Fate or to God: the decision whether or not to do right rests mainly with men, but in every action Fate takes some part. Every soul is imperishable, but only the souls of good men pass into other bodies, the souls of bad men being subject to eternal punishment.

The Sadducees, the second order, deny fate altogether and hold that God is incapable of either committing sin or seeing it; they say that men are free to choose between good and evil, and each must decide which he will follow.

The permanence of the soul, punishments in Hades and rewards they deny utterly. Again, Pharisees are friendly to one another and seek to promote concord with the general public, but Sadducees, even towards each other, show a more disagreeable spirit, and in their relations with men like themselves they are as harsh as they might be towards foreigners. (pp.133, 137-8)

The Essenes profess a severer discipline; they are Jews by birth and are peculiarly attached to each other... Their rule is that novices admitted to the sect must surrender their property to the order, so that among them all neither humiliating poverty nor excessive wealth is ever seen,... but as with brothers their entire property belongs to them all....

They possess no one city but everywhere have large colonies. When adherents arrive from elsewhere, all local resources are put at their disposal as if they were their own... And so when they travel they carry no baggage at all, but only weapons to keep off bandits.... (After the morning work) they again meet in one place and donning loin cloths wash all over in cold water... They then go into the refectory in a state of ritual cleanliness as if it were a holy temple and sit down in silence.... The priest says the grace before meat: to taste food before this prayer is forbidden. After breakfast he offers a second prayer; for at the beginning and the end they give thanks to God as the Giver of life.

It is indeed their unshakeable conviction that bodies are corruptible and the material composing them impermanent, whereas souls remain immortal for ever. (pp.133, 134, 136)

There was a further party known as the Zealots, hated by Josephus, who were extreme nationalists, described by Josephus in his later work, "The Antiquities of the Jews", 93AD.

Of the fourth sect of Jewish philosophy, Judas the Galilean (c. 6AD) was the author. These men agree in all other things with Pharisaic notions, but they have an inviolable attachment to liberty, and say that God is to be their only Ruler and Lord.

They also do not value dying any kinds of death, nor do they heed the deaths of their relatives and friends ... and it was in Gessius Florus' time (66-68AD) that the nation began to grow mad with this distemper.. (p. 775)

Sadducees (as seen by Pharisees)

Yohanan ben Zakai said:

> *"Guard your steps when you go to the house of God.*
> *To draw near to listen is better than to offer the sacrifice*
> *of fools, for they do not know they are doing evil."*
> *(N p.44)*

Woe unto me because of the house of Boethus
Woe unto me because of their clubs! ...
Woe unto me because of the house of Ishmael ben Phiabi,
Woe unto me because of their fists! ...
For they are high priests
And their sons are treasurers
And their sons-in-law are law officers,
And their slaves beat the folk with sticks.
(N p.36)

Pharisees

The great rabbi Hillel (100BC – c10AD?) was asked to recite the whole Law while standing on one leg. He said,

> *"What is hateful to you, do not do to your fellow: this is the whole Torah; the rest is the explanation; go and learn."*

He also said,

> *"Whoever has acquired the words of the Law*
> *has acquired the life of the world to come."*

and

> *"If I am not for myself, who will be for me?*
> *And if I am only for myself, who am I?*
> *And if not now, when?"*

Yohanan ben Zakkai was said to have studied under Hillel. He went on to found a Jewish academy after the destruction of Jerusalem which proved essential for the continuation of Jewish life. He died about 80AD.

They tell of Rabban Yohanan ben Zakkai that he did not neglect a single Scripture or Mishnah, Gemara (interpretation of Mishnah), halakah (law), agada (legend), supplement (branch of oral law), or the subtleties of Scripture, or the subtleties of the scribes, or any of the sages' rules of interpretation..."
(N p.26)

For the Pharisees the Torah or law included both the first five books of the Old Testament and later interpretation.

Agrippa the Prince asked R Yohanan ben Zakkai, "How many Torahs does he give you from heaven." He answered him, "Two, one in writing and one to be transmitted orally."
(N p.171)

Paul gives a good example of Pharisaic interpretation in 1 Corinthians 9.2-10:

> *"Do we not have a right to food and drink?.... Do I say this on human authority? Does not the Law say the same? For it is written in the Law of Moses, "You shall not muzzle an ox while it is treading out the grain." Is it of oxen that God is concerned? Or does he not speak entirely for our sake?..."*

For Pharisees, the Torah equated to the Wisdom of God:

The Torah says, I was God's instrument. According to the custom of the world... an architect does not build (a palace) out of his own head but employs plans and diagrams... So too did the Holy One, blessed be He, He looked into the Torah and created the world. (N. p.65)

It is said that Yohanan ben Zakkai prophesied the destruction of the Temple:

Forty years before the destruction of the temple... the doors of the sanctuary opened by themselves, until Rabban Yohanan ben Zakkai rebuked them saying, "Oh Temple, Temple! Why do you yourself give the alarm? I know about you that you will be destroyed..." (N. p.39)

When Rabban ben Zakkai heard that Jerusalem was destroyed, and the Temple was up in flames, he tore his clothing and his disciples tore their clothing, and they wept, crying aloud and mourning." (N. p.128)

One of R Yohanan ben Zakkai's disciples was R Eliezer. He was deeply conservative and was eventually excommuicated, suffering a melancholy old age. Here are some of his sayings:

"Let the honour of thy fellow be as dear to thee as thine own. Be not easily angered. Repent one day before thy death"

"Keep warm at the fire of the sages, but beware of their glowing coals lest thou be scorched, for their bite is as the bite of the jackal, and their sting the sting of a scorpion. Moreover all their words are like coals of fire."
(N p. 76)

Essenes
From the manual of Discipline, Dead Sea Scrolls:

This is the regulation for the men of the commune, who devote themselves to turn away from all evil, and to hold fast to all that He has commanded as His will, to separate themselves from the congregation of the men of iniquity, to be a commune in Torah and property. (N. p.11)

Charismatic Judaism
There was another stream of Judaism at the time of Jesus which was centred in Galilee, a more charismatic and relational expression of faith. It caused R Yohanan ben Zakkai to exclaim, *"Galilee, Galilee, you hate the Torah! Your end will be to be besieged!" (N. p.29)*

R Yohanan had only one student from Galilee, Hanina ben Dosa who shows this:

> *When the son of Gamaliel I was ill, he sent two disciples to Hanina to ask his prayers in the boy's behalf. When Hanina saw them, he went to the upper chamber of his house and prayed for mercy. When he came down he said to the disciples, "Go, for the fever has left him."*
>
> *"And are you a prophet?" they asked.*
>
> *"I am neither a prophet or a son of a prophet, but I am accustomed to discern thus: if the prayer is fluent in my mouth, I know that it is accepted, and if not, I know that it is rejected."*
>
> *One day a "heavenly echo" came forth and announced, "All the world is fed on account of Hanina my son, and Hanina my son suffices on a basket of carobs from week to week."*
> *(N. p. 29-30)*

A century earlier another miracle worker, probably also from Galilee, is recorded:

> *Once they said to Honi the Circle-drawer: "Pray that it may rain." ... He prayed and it did not rain. Then what did he do? He drew a circle and stood in it and said before God: "Lord of the world, thy children have turned to me because I am as a son of the house before thee. I swear by thy great name that I will not move hence until thou be merciful to- wards thy children." It then began to drizzle. "I have not asked for this," he said, "but for rain to fill cisterns, pits and rock-cavities."*

Month 5: Jesus

> There came a cloudburst. "I have not asked for this, but for a rain of grace, blessing and gift." It then rained normally.

A leading Pharisee commented:

> What can I do with you, since even though you importune God, he does what you wish in the same way that a father does whatever his importuning son asks him?
> (G. Vermes: Jesus the Jew p.70)

MONTH 6
THE APOSTLES & THEIR LETTERS

What happened after Jesus' resurrection? Luke wrote a second volume after his Gospel to answer just that, the Acts of the Apostles.

The first 12 chapters give a series of snapshots of the new Jesus community based in Jerusalem, including the coming of the Holy Spirit at Pentecost, increased persecution and the first outreach to the Gentiles – those outside the Jewish community. The remaining 14 chapters follow St Paul in his missionary journeys across modern Turkey and Greece, and ending up as a state prisoner in Rome.

What effect did the gospel – this strange good news that the apostles proclaimed - have on people's lives? And what does it mean for us?

The letters written by the apostles give penetrating insights into our human need, God's actions through Jesus to address it, and the new way of living which issues from it.
A key problem was how Jewish and Gentile Christians could live peaceably together without either forcing Gentile believers to become Jews or devaluing the religious lifestyle which for Jews symbolised obedience to God.

Over half of the letters are from Paul, and we look at his two major ones, 1 Corinthians and Romans. 1 Corinthians was written to new, enthusiastic but problematic Christians.

Month 6: The Apostles and their Letters

Romans is a powerful statement of the Christian faith, one which has had a revolutionary impact on Christians down the centuries. In week 4 we sample the shorter letters, including one from James, the Lord's brother, Peter, John, and the visionary book of Revelation – all written before 100 AD.

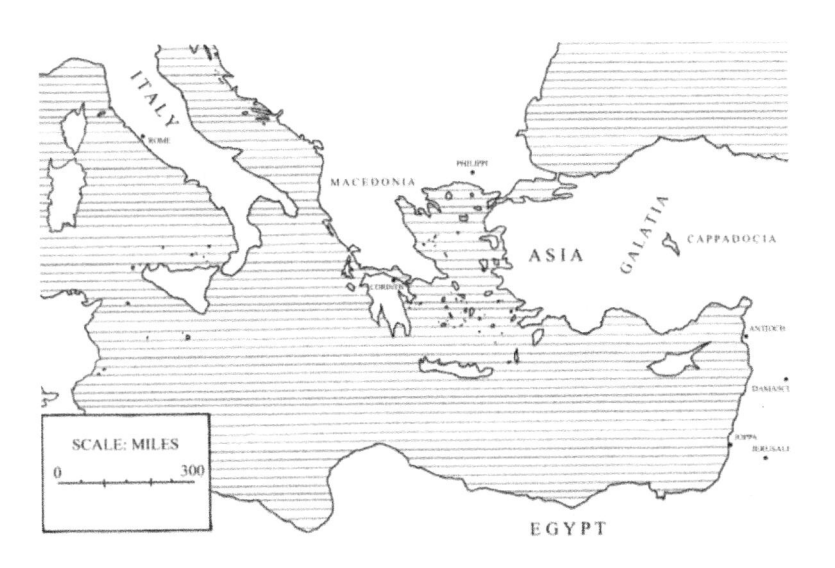

The eastern Roman Empire

MONTH 6 WEEK 1
ACTS OF THE APOSTLES

Day 1   Acts 1.1-14 The promise of the Spirit
What were the disciples waiting for, and what did Jesus want them to wait for?

Day 2   Act 2 The coming of the Spirit
Why were the crowd "cut to the heart"? (v.37)
What did Peter promise?

Day 3   Act 4 Threat of persecution
What gave the first believers such courage?
Note: Peter and John were arrested after healing a crippled beggar in the temple, and then preaching to the crowd about Jesus. (Acts 3)

Day 4   Acts 9.1-31 The call of Saul (Paul)
Note 1: Saul was already a violent persecutor of the followers of Jesus, see Acts 8.1-3.
Note 2: Saul is better known by his Roman name Paul, the name he would have used outside Palestine.
Saul had a complete change of heart; from what to what?
(See Philippians 3.4-11)

Day 5   Act 10 The first Gentile Christian
In this chapter, how many times did God take the initiative to bring the message of Jesus to the non-Jewish world?

Month 6: The Apostles and their Letters

READ   **RESPOND**   **REFLECT**   **RECORD**

"God has raised this Jesus to life,
and we are all witnesses of the fact."
Acts 2.32

BIBLE IN BRIEF

Day 6   Act 15 Facing the danger of disunity
Note: The Gospel was spread to the Gentiles by
   a) the scattering of Jerusalem converts through persecution there (Acts 11.19-26), and
   b) the missionary journeys of Paul & Barnabas.
Genesis 17.14 states, "Any uncircumcised male ... shall be cut off from his people; he has broken my covenant."
What caused the early church to ignore this commandment?

Day 7   Acts 16.11-40 Paul at Philippi
Note: Luke joined Paul at v.10 ("they" changes to "we"). From here Luke is a first hand witness.
Imagine you are a magistrate in Philippi.
Write out a "Wanted" notice for St Paul.

"Alexamenos worships his god." "Alexamenos is faithfull"
Anti-Christian graffiti 4th century Rome

Month 6: The Apostles and their Letters

READ   **RESPOND**   **REFLECT**   **RECORD**

"So then, God has granted even the
Gentiles repentance unto life."
Acts 11.18

MONTH 6 WEEK 2
PAUL'S LETTER TO NEW CHRISTIANS c. 55 AD

Day 1   1 Corinthians 1 Unity and the cross
What does Paul feel most passionately about?
Note: Letters in Roman times always began:
x to y – thanksgiving - the letter itself – farewell greeting. The New Testament letters follow exactly the same pattern.

Day 2   1 Corinthians 6 Property and sexual ethics
Paul's ethics are as radical as Jesus': "Why not rather be wronged?" (v.7) "Your body is a temple of the Holy Spirit." (v.19) How can we grow into such attitudes? Do we want to?

Day 3   1 Corinthians 7 Marriage
Paul's concern is not to burden Christians but to cultivate a certain detachment from this world. But does he fail to see how different experiences can help us grow in love?

Day 4   1 Corinthians 11.17-end The Lord's Supper
In Paul's time Holy Communion, was more like a communal meal than a church service. What were the benefits and the pitfalls?

Day 5   1 Corinthians 12 Spiritual gifts and unity
The Christians in Corinth were proud of their supernatural worship gifts. Paul stresses that the main point must be unity and service. How is the church like/unlike the "body of Christ"?

Month 6: The Apostles and their Letters

| READ | RESPOND | REFLECT | RECORD |

Paul ... to the church of God in Corinth,
to those sanctified in Christ Jesus
and called to be holy...
Grace and peace to you from God our Father
and the Lord Jesus Christ.
1 Corinthians 1.1-3

Day 6   1 Corinthians 13 The greatest is love
The most famous chapter of the Bible. But try replacing the word "love" with the word "I"!

Day 7   1 Corinthians 15 Christ's resurrection and ours
Paul makes three main points here:
　　1 Christ really was raised from death.
　　2 Resurrection is now our birthright.
　　3 Our future body will be completely different -
　　　"a spiritual body", but with complete continuity.
Does it make sense?

Couple from Pompei

Month 6: The Apostles and their Letters

READ   **RESPOND**   **REFLECT**   **RECORD**

And now these three remain: faith, hope and love.
But the greatest of these is love.
1 Corinthians 13.13

MONTH 6 WEEK 3
PAUL'S LETTER TO CHRISTIANS IN ROME
c. 57 AD

Day 1   Romans 1 Introduction & the ills of society
Note: Paul's aim is to win friends in the Roman church, so he starts with a standard Jewish attack on pagan society.
What are the consequences for society of a widespread loss of faith?

Day 2   Romans 3 "There is no difference"
Paul's argument goes in four stages:
- v.1-4   The value of the Jewish covenant
- v.5-9   Paul's rejection of the charge that relying on faith leads to moral anarchy.
- v.10-20 Proof texts from the Old Testament to show that Jews as much as Gentiles are under God's judgement.
- v.21-26 Jesus has broken through the impasse which separates men and women from God – see note 2 which follows.
- v.27-31 Summary of the argument

Note 1: The Jewish faith offered a radical and Impressive alternative to Greek and Roman religion – an ethical and spiritual religion as against a religion made up of community ritual & sympathetic magic – akin to Hinduism today.

Note 2: In talking of Christ's work on the cross, Paul uses language from the law court (justification), the slave market (redemption), the temple (sacrifice) (3.24-25), and the family (reconciliation) (5.10)

Month 6: The Apostles and their Letters

READ **RESPOND** **REFLECT** **RECORD**

In the gospel a righteousness from God is revealed,
a righteousness that is by faith from first to last,
just as it is written *"The righteous will live by faith."*
Romans 1.17

Note 3: The same Greek word means both righteousness and justice/justification. The basic meaning is of being set right.

When I focus on the cross of Christ, does it enable me to open up to God in a new way? Or not?

Day 3   Romans 5.1-11 Reconciled to God in Christ
"While we were yet sinners, Christ died for us."
What, in Paul's account, are the results for us?

Day 4   Romans 6 Dead to sin, alive to Christ
What, for Paul, is the basis of Christian morality?

Day 5   Romans 7.7-25 The struggle with sin
Does this ring any bells?

Day 6 Romans 8.1-17 New life in the Spirit
Note 1: When Paul talks about "the flesh", he does not mean our physical body. (That is a different word). He means our natural self-centredness or ego. (Some translations use the term "sinful nature").
Note 2: To "live by the Spirit" is to experience an "entire psychic change" through which we become God-centred instead of self-centred.
What is attractive about Paul's vision for human life?

Month 6: The Apostles and their Letters

READ **RESPOND** **REFLECT** **RECORD**

All have sinned and fall short of the glory of God,
and are justified freely by his grace.
Romans 3:23-24

BIBLE IN BRIEF

Day 7   Romans 12 Practical Christian life
"Be transformed..."
What parts of Paul's counsel do we welcome, what parts do we find difficult?

Woman praying, from Pompeii

Month 6: The Apostles and their Letters

READ	RESPOND	REFLECT	RECORD

Because you are sons (and daughters*),
God sent the Spirit of his Son into our hearts,
the Spirit who calls out "Abba, Father".
Galatians 4.6 (*added)

MONTH 6 WEEK 4
OTHER LETTERS

Day 1   Colossians 1.1-20 Christ, the image of God
Paul talks as if Christ is the Wisdom of God (see Proverbs 8), Is this a helpful thought?

Day 2   Ephesians 4 Live as children of light
Paul urges us to "Grow up!" What could be our next step – as individuals or as a church?

Day 3   Hebrews 12 "Don't give up!"
Note: A message to Jewish Christians who are at risk of relapsing. The passage refers back to Exodus 19, the Israelites facing God at Mount Sinai.
What is the writer's view of God?

Day 4   James 1 The godly lifestyle
Note: Probably written by James (or Jacob) the brother of Jesus and leader of the church in Jerusalem. It reflects a Palestinian approach to following Jesus.
Perseverance – faith – humility – sober speech attentiveness – helping the poor.
Do we know a group showing these characteristics?

Day 5   1 Peter 1.1-11, 2.1-10 A living hope
Note: Probably written from Rome to persecuted churches in what is now Turkey.
Hope. Faith. Love. Choose a sentence which reflects each of these.

Month 6: The Apostles and their Letters

READ **RESPOND** **REFLECT** **RECORD**

Be imitators of God, as dearly loved children,
and live a life of love,
just as Christ loved us and gave himself
up for us as a fragrant offering and sacrifice to God.
Ephesians 5.1,2

Day 6   1 John 4.7-21 God is love
What, for John, is the best example of love?

Day 7   Revelation 1 + 21.1-7
         A vision of Christ and future glory
Note 1: After the destruction of the Temple in 66 AD, several Jewish Apocalypses described God's judgement. 'Revelation' is the only Christian example.
Note 2: John was a Jewish Christian church leader, sentenced in 95 AD to be a state slave in the stone quarries of Patmos, a small island near Turkey.
Note 3: Revelation was not finally accepted into the Bible by the whole church until after 400 AD.
How could the vision of Christ in glory and of the heavenly city encourage a church suffering persecution?

Christ the good shepherd, Ravenna 6th century

Month 6: The Apostles and their Letters

READ **RESPOND** **REFLECT** **RECORD**

To him who loves us
and has freed us from our sins by his blood,
and has made us to be a kingdom and priests
to serve his God and Father —
to him be glory and power
for ever and ever! Amen.
Revelation 1: 5,6

THE OTHER SIDE
ROMAN REACTIONS

The reaction of the average citizen of the Romand Empire to this new semi-Jewish sect was uniformly negative. All quotations are taken from "A New Eusebius", ed. J Stevenson.

In July 64 there was a disastrous fire in Rome which destroyed two thirds of the city. The emperor Nero was popularly blamed. The Roman historian Tacitus wrote about it fifty years later:

To get rid of this report, Nero fastened the guilt and inflicted the most exquisite tortures on a class hated for their abominations by the populace... Christus, from whom the name had its origin, suffered the extreme penalty during the reign of Tiberius at the hand of one of our procurators, Pontius Pilate, and a deadly superstition, thus checked for the moment, again broke out, not only in Judaea, the first source of the evil, but also in the City (i.e. Rome) where all things hideous and shameful from every part of the world meet and become popular. Accordingly, an arrest was first made of all who confessed; then, upon their information, an immense multitude was convicted, not so much of the crime of arson, as of hatred of the human race... Covered with the skins of beasts, they were torn by dogs and perished, or were nailed to crosses, or were doomed to the flames .... (ANE p.2)

The younger Pliny was Governor of Bithynia around 112 AD, and he wrote to the Emperor Trajan asking his advice to see if he had acted correctly. The emperor said he had.

This is the course I have taken with those who were accused before me as Christians. I asked them if they were Christians, and if they confessed, I asked them a second and a third time with threats of punishment. If they kept to it, I ordered them for execution... There were others of the like insanity; but as these were Roman citizens, I noted them down to be sent to Rome...

An unsigned paper was presented, which gave the names of many. As for those who said that they neither were nor ever had been Christians, I thought it right to let them go, since they recited a prayer to the gods at my dictation, made supplication with incense and wine to your statue... and moreover cursed Christ – things which (so it is said) those who are really Christians cannot be made to do.

Others who were named by the informer said they had been Christians and then denied it, explaining that they had been, but had ceased to be such, some three years ago, some a good many years, and a few even twenty. All these too both worshipped your statue and the images of the gods, and cursed Christ.

They maintained, however, that the amount of their fault or error had been this, that it was their habit on a fixed day to assemble before daylight and recite by turns a form of words to Christ as a god; and that they bound themselves with an oath, not for any crime, but not to commit theft or robbery or adultery, not to break their word, and not to deny a deposit when demanded. After this, their custom was to depart, and to meet again to take food, but ordinary and harmless food; and even this (they said) they had given up doing after the issue of my edict, by which in accordance with your commands, I had forbidden the existence of clubs...

The matter seemed to me worth deliberation, especially on account of the number of those in danger; for many of all age and every rank, and also of both sexes are brought into present and future danger.. The contagion of that superstition has penetrated not the cities only, but the villages and the country; yet it seems to me possible to to stop it and set it right. At any rate it is certain enough that the almost deserted temples begin to be resorted to, that long disused ceremonies of religion are restored, and that fodder for (animal) victims finds a market, whereas buyers till now were very few. From this it may easily be supposed, what a multitude of men can be reclaimed, if there be a place of repentance. (ANE p. 12-13)

Note: The Christian faith was illegal from the time of Nero's persecution in 64 AD up to the Edict of Milan by the co-Emperors Constantine and Licinius in 313 AD.

Bonus Features

The World's Greatest Book?	166
Chapter and Verse	169
Which Bible?	170
Scientists on the Bible	173
Film recommendations	174
Illustrations	179
What has been missed out?	181
Andrew Roland - a brief biography	182

The World's Greatest Book?

It's a bit of a claim, isn't it?

And one for which I have to claim responsibility. After all, I chose to put it on the front cover of this book. Can I justify it?

The Word of God

Most Christians would happily refer to the Bible as the Word of God. Those who worship at churches using liturgy (set forms of prayers) such as the Roman Catholic and Anglican churches regularly use a response after readings from the Bible:

> *This is the word of the Lord*
> *Thanks be to God.*

But what do they mean by it? A divine document? Some Christians point to a verse in a letter ascribed to the apostle Paul, 2 Timothy 3.16: *"All Scripture is God-breathed/inspired and is useful for teaching, rebuking, correcting and training in righteousness..."*

The problem with this is threefold. First, it is hard for someone to be a witness in their own cause. Secondly, when this was written, it referred not to what we know as the New Testament which had not been formed then, but to the Hebrew scriptures, possibly including the Apocrypha; and for Christians the most important part of the Bible they look to is the New Testament. Thirdly, the verse describes the Scriptures as practically useful in leading a godly life, not as a standard of absolute truth. So where do we go from here?

It seems to me that there are six possible approaches.

1 A divine document
Every word was dictated by God, and so every sentence can be literally applied to us, at least in a spiritual sense.

But this takes no account of the wide variety of voices and types of writing we find in the Bible. It actually reflects what Muslims believe about the Koran rather than a Christian approach.

2 A divine-human document
The message of each part of the Bible is divinely authored, but expressed through the human personality of the writer. This leads us to interpret each part of the Bible as a subset of an overarching message, a message of salvation and transformation open to everyone.

a) Lightning flashes
Human beings wrote it for their own times, using their best understanding. But sometimes God breaks through and inspires them to write universal truth. For instance, chapter 13 of Paul's first letter to the Christians at Corinth which begins, *"Though I speak in the tongues of men and of angels, but have not love, I am only a resounding gong or a clanging cymbal..."*

Yet only two chapters before, Paul is telling them off for allowing women to come to worship without covering their heads. A friend of mine heard that passage read in church, very eloquently, by a woman churchwarden, who concluded by saying, *"I am not going to say 'This is the word of the Lord. It is just St Paul being silly."*

b) Divine infection

The books of the Bible were written by human beings, but they were close enough to the actual moments of divine encounter as to be trustworthy carriers of the original message or event, and something of the spiritual power of these events flavours their accounts. The gospels are a case in point. This was the approach taken by the early church who accepted books into the canon of the New Testament if they were believed to be by the original apostles.

c) A channel for God

However it came to be written it has always been a channel by which God has addressed people personally. One story is of Anthony Bloom, the Russian Orthodox Archbishop. As a rebellious teenager in Paris, a friend pleaded with him to accompany him to hear a preacher which the lad's parents wanted him to hear. What Anthony heard made him so angry that he decided to be done with Christianity for ever. Just to make sure, he decided to read one gospel and then finish with the faith. He chose Mark because it was the shortest and he did not want to waste more time than necessary. He sat at his desk and began to read. While he was reading chapter four he knew that Jesus was standing on the other side of the desk, and it changed his life.

3 A human document

At the most basic level, the Bible is a record of human experience covering over 1,500 years, the good, the bad and the ugly. As the News of the World used to proclaim (about itself) "All human life is there." And crucially it includes the gospels which tell of Jesus - the most powerful stories the world has heard. There is literally no book to compare with it.

Explore!

Chapter and Verse

The Bible's Search Engine

When the Hebrew and Greek parts of the Bible were written, the only divisions were spaces between paragraphs, and that continued for over a thousand years. The only way to really know your way around the Bible was to memorise large chunks of it (see Luke 4.17). It was our own Archbishop of Canterbury, Stephen Langton, famous for helping make King John sign the Magna Carta, who divided the Bible into chapters. This was in 1205, and his system has been adopted by the church all over the world.

With numbered chapters, it became much easier to go to particular stories or large passages. But if you wanted to find a specific phrase or sentence you need much smaller divisions. Isaac Nathan ben Kalonymus, a French Jew, divided the Old Testament in this way around 1440, and a French protestant, Robert Estienne, did the same for the New Testament in Geneva in 1551.

We can now find any particular passage quite easily. Mark 14.27-50 means Mark chapter 14, verses 27 to 50. Mark 14.51-15.15 means Mark chapter 14 verse 51 to chapter 15 verse 15.

Modern editors also put subheadings in, *usually in italics*. It stops the Bible from just being a forbidding block of text and helps us follow the argument of the book we are reading. But they are not part of Scripture, just the editor's ideas.

Which Bible?

When the future American church leader John Wimber first became a Christian, he was told by a friend that he needed to get a proper Bible. A "proper" Bible was the "King James Virgin". Quite apart from this hilarious error, John Wimber's friend was wrong.

There are over 30 different translations of the Bible available, all of them in more up to date English than the King James Version, published 1611. Some of them try to translate the Greek and Hebrew as accurately as possible, others try to paraphrase the meaning in contemporary language. Some translations make their version as gender-neutral as possible, such as the NRSV, (though none go as far as translating the Lord's Prayer as "Our Parent who are in heaven").

Here are thirteen popular versions. In November 2014 I found that I could get each of them second hand on Amazon for 1p plus postage – apart from the Anglo Saxon manuscript of the Wessex Gospels.

Bonus Features

Fæder ure þu þe eart on heofonum, si þin nama gehalgod.
990 AD the Wessex Gospels

After thys maner therefore pray ye, O oure father which arte in heve hallowed by thy name.
William Tyndale 1526

After this manner therefore pray ye: Our Father which art in heaven, Hallowed be thy name.
King James Version (KJV) 1611

Pray then like this: Our Father who art in heaven, Hallowed be thy name.
Revised Standard Version (RSV) 1946 New Testament only, 1952 the whole Bible

"This is how you should pray: Our Father in heaven, thy name be hallowed."
New English Bible (NEB) 1961 New Testament, 1970 the whole Bible

This, then, is how you should pray: "Our Father in heaven: May your holy name be honoured;"
Good News Bible 1966 New Testament only, 1976 the whole Bible

"This, then, is how you should pray: " 'Our Father in heaven, hallowed be your name,"
New International Version (NIV) 1973

In this manner, therefore, pray: Our Father in heaven, Hallowed be Your name.
New King James Version (NKJV) 1982

"Pray then in this way: Our Father in heaven, hallowed be your name."
New Revised Standard Version (NRSV) 1989 Note: Some editions include the Apocrypha.

So you should pray like this: Our Father in heaven, may your name be held holy.
Jerusalem Bible 1966.
Note: this is a Roman Catholic Bible and includes the Apocrypha. Also, it uses the probable name for God in the Old Testament, "Yahweh" (formerly Jehovah) where other translations use "LORD" in capitals.

"This is how you should pray. " 'Our Father in heaven, may your name be honoured.'"
New International Revised Version (NIRV) 1995

Pray then like this: "Our Father in heaven, hallowed be your name."
English Standard Version (ESV) 2001

With a God like this loving you, you can pray very simply. Like this: Our Father in heaven, Reveal who you are.
The Message 2002

Most of these versions are also available on the internet. For example, www.biblegateway.org

Scientists on the Bible

"This book is an inexhaustible source of life, wisdom and faith. Read often from it and think of him through it."
Einstein, 1932 written on the flyleaf of a Bible given to an American friend.

"The Bible (is) a collection of honourable but still primitive legends and are nevertheless pretty childish".
Einstein 1954

"The Bible should be taught, but emphatically not as reality. It is fiction, myth, poetry, anything but reality. As such it needs to be taught because it underlies so much of our literature and culture."
Richard Dawkins

"I think we should all read the Bible, and I believe in the priesthood of the believer. It's biblical to do so; it's certainly the way that Christ seems to be teaching us, but that means responsibility to read the Bible at more than the most superficial level.

"Curious believers will want to go deeper, but that deeper searching has to involve more than searching through the Bible. We must also search through the other book that God gave us - the book of nature."
Francis Collins, Director of the Human Genome Project, 1993 - 2008

Film recommendations

Films can be an excellent way into the Bible, but they can be cringe-making, boring, weird, too American or just plain wrong. Here are the films I would personally recommend (and some I would not). It is not an exhaustive list by any means.

The Old Testament

I have yet to see a full-length film on the Old Testament that works. I remember sitting through John Huston's **"The Bible – In the Beginning"** in 1966 and wondering how such a renowned director could make so tedious a picture.

I would not take seriously the cheesy Cecil B de Mille's **"The Ten Commandments"** (1956) except as a fascinating bit of Hollywood history. It is memorable, but not in a good way, e.g. Yul Brynner's (Pharaoh's) immortal line "His God – is God". Nor would I recommend the Spielberg's animation film on Moses: **"The Prince of Egypt"** (1998) - it soft soaps the story like later Disney; so Moses' murder of an Egyptian supervisor becomes just an unfortunate accident.

Streets ahead of anything I have seen is the DVD **"Testament - The Bible in Animation"** (1996). It covers nine key figures of the Old Testament in 25 minute episodes – brilliantly scripted and created with wonderful imagination.

It started out as a series on BBC2 in 1996, a Welsh/Russian co-production. The Moses episode won the Outstanding Achievement in Animation award at Primetime Emmy- it has a great script and expressionist drawing. The Moses and Joseph episodes were both nominated for the BAFA award for the best animated short film. For many years you could only get it on VHS format, the copyright owners being apparently unwilling to put it on DVD.

For a short time it was available from the Bible Society (www.biblesociety.org), but this is no longer the case. However, they are all available on youtube! See link at bibleinbrief.org

The New Testament

The people who produced "Testament" went on to make "**The Miracle Maker**"(1999), the story of Jesus taken largely from the gospel of Luke. It uses 3D puppets for the main story with pastel-crayon drawing for parables and the inner life of Jesus.

The script is fantastic, full of humour and real human interactions, and a clear telling of the story. I have used it countless times in the parish without encountering any cringe factors.

The Time Out review described it as "Strange - and strangely compelling".

Three other versions should be mentioned.

"**The Gospel according to St Matthew**" (1964) is a black and white film of the named gospel made by the great Italian communist director Pasolini as a tribute to Pope John XXIII.. It is a literal portrayal of the gospel on film - bleak and powerful and strange. To be seen, but not too often. The film is available on www.youtube.com

"**Jesus**" or "**The Jesus film**" (1979) is an explicitly evangelistic project, to film the gospel of Luke. It is a good straightforward account, made to be seen by as many people around the world as possible. Over the last 25 years it has been shown in every country on earth and has been dubbed into over 1,200 languages. I saw it one Easter weekend being shown on Iranian state television! The website is www.jesusfilm.org. For a direct link see www.bibleinbrief.org

Zeffirelli's "**Jesus of Nazareth**" (1977) was made as a television series and lasts 6½ hours. It bears all the hallmarks of Zeffirelli's work – amazing crowd scenes, great sense of drama, long "meaningful" shots of countryside, and long intense gazes.

You do get a real sense of first century Palestine as a place where people actually lived and struggled with life. Robert Powell as Jesus does get a bit starry-eyed at times – helped by the swelling orchestra in the background – not quite a man's man.

When the teenage Jesus' bar mitzvah was being filmed, the young actor stumbled over the reading of the Hebrew scriptures."Cut!" shouted Zeffirelli."But, Mr Zeffirelli," commented the Jewish adviser - actually the rabbi of the West London synagogue, "every Jewish boy stumbles while reading the Torah at his bar mitzvah." "Notta the Son of God" announced the director.

Where it stands out is in the secondary characters: Peter Usti-nov as Herod, showing all the sinister sense of humour of a psychopath, Christopher Plummer as the younger Herod with a playboy's view of life, and an amazing portrayal of Pilate by Rod Steiger. It is available on youtube.

And not appearing:

I saw two films in the '60s. "**King of kings**" (1961) had Jeffrey Hunter as an all-American Christ. In "**The Greatest Story Ever Told**" (1965) Max von Sydow brought Swedish intensity to the part of Jesus. It is amazingly slow and ponderous, lasting over 4 hours, and only to be recommended for people suffering seriously from insomnia. If advised by your doctor, it is available on youtube.

One story, apocryphal or not, has the director advising John Wayne, playing the Roman centurion at the cross.

"When you say, "Truly, this man was the son of God", I want you to say it with awe."
"OK, I got you ."
"Action!"
"Aw, truly this man was the son of God".

Both of them struck me as basically safe religious films. I think you need more than 'safe'.

"**The Passion of the Christ**" (2004) by Mel Gibson is not safe, it is a truly horrific piece of work. Its gratuitous violence and its use of a kind of creepy horror to drive the story along makes it "tough to sit through and obscures whatever message it is trying to convey." (Rotten Tomatoes) A notable feature of the film is that it is spoken entirely in Hebrew and Latin.

This certainly creates a disturbing sense of otherness and of a completely different culture from ours. Unfortunately the version on youtube (yes, you can get it on youtube) leaves out the subtitles!

For Christmas

There was a wonderful four part series on the birth of Jesus by the BBC in 2011 called "**Nativity**". It uses the Biblical material to create believable situations. Very good indeed.

Bonus Features

Illustrations

Map of the Middle East	14
Impression of the ziggurat of Ur in present day Iraq – a temple on a man-made hill	24
A family of the Aamu of North Arabia, Egyptian wall-painting	28
War captives building the temple of Amun c 1450 BC	32
Mount Sinai	36
Assyria god Nisroch	39, 41
Canaanite pottery coffins c1400 BC found near Gaza	46
Israelite altar from Beer-sheva 11th - 9th century BC	50
Jehu of Israel submitting to king Shalmaneser III of Assyria 841 BC, from the obelisk in the British Museum	54
War captives being led into exhile	58
Isiah scroll from the Dead Sea Scrolls	66
Ivory furniture decorations from Kinf Ahab's palace in Samaria c 800 BC	70
The Kaiser Wilhelm Memorial Church, Berlin, built 1891 bombed 1943. The quotation is from the plaque on the tower.	74
The Ishtar gate, Babylon, built 575 BC Persian Warrior	78
A Persian Warrior	82

BIBLE IN BRIEF

Nergal, Babylonian god of war and death	87
The shofar or rams horn in a call to worship	92
Egyptian musicians from a wall painting in the tomb of Rameses III 1155 BC	94
An Egyptian scribe, 3000 to 1700 BC. It took at least 4 years training to become a scribe.	98
Jerusalem tombs c. 2nd century BC	102
Temple of Solomon	110
Map of Palestine at the time of Jesus	115
Bethlehem around 1950	118
Capernaum at the time of Jesus	120
Herod's Temple at the time of Jesus. The Antonia Tower for the Roman garrison is on the right.	124
The hill of Golgotha, outside the city wall	128
Palestinian women grinding coffee	132
Map of the Roman Empire	143
Anti-Christian graffiti in the quarters of the imperial pages at the Palatine, Rome 3rd Century	146
Couple from Pompei	150
Woman praying from Pompei, before 79 AD	156
The Good Shepherd from mosaic in Ravenna c 400 AD	160

What has been missed out?

Out of the 66 named books of the Bible, 24 have not put in an appearance. 16 are quite short, with 6 chapters or less:

- Ruth - the romantic story of David's great-grandmother
- 5 of the 12 minor prophets: Joel (but not if you count the quotation in Acts 2), Obadiah, Nahum, Habbakuk, and Zephaniah
- Galatians - the most personal of all Paul's letters
- 1 & 2 Thessalonians - the earliest of Paul's letters
- 1 & 2 Timothy, Titus - written while Paul was in prison though their authenticity is questioned
- Philemon - a simple private letter of Paul to a friend
- 2 Peter - unlikely to be by Peter, accepted very late
- 2 & 3 John - two very short letters – only 27 verses
- Jude - a short, fierce letter by the little known apostle

The longer books which have been omitted are:

1 & 2 Chronicles
Lists of names, followed by a retelling of 2 Samuel and 1 & 2 Kings but "airbrushed" after the exile to iron out moral ambiguities.

Ezra
A contemporary account of the return from exile and the re-establishment of the Jewish religion.

Esther
A tale of persecution and turning the tables

2 Corinthians
A compilation of three passionate letters from Paul

Andy Roland

A brief biography

I was born in the last few days of the Second World War, and into 6 years of food rationing. My father had been a refugee from Nazi Germany; he became a doctor and eventually an ENT consultant. He married my mother, a Christian, during the war; since they wanted me to choose my own religion, I was baptised with my own agreement when I was 8. I spent four years in boarding school and prayer became important to me. When I was 11 my parents wanted to go to Uganda, where my father would set up an ENT speciality. They asked me if it was OK by me for them to go. I said it was fine and even offered to do a paper round to help pay for it! I had some great holidays out there, seeing elephants, lions etc in the wild, and swimming in the Indian Ocean. I had a wonderful education at Rugby School, where I was a day boy, and also got involved in a local church youth club where I made some really good friendships.

I read history at Merton College, Oxford – such a privilege – and also made an important new step of committing myself to God, taking prayer and Bible reading much more seriously, and getting involved in the life of St Aldate's, an open evangelical church in Oxford.

I was thinking of being ordained as a priest in the Church of England, but decided I should see a bit more of life first. There followed two years in two secondary modern schools in Coventry and Birmingham where I taught history and RE – which certainly got rid of some of the wet behind my ears. It was at that time that I came to the conclusion that being a vicar was a very odd calling, one which I was not sure I had then, and the bishop of Coventry agreed with me. This was followed by taking the Diploma in Personnel Management at Aston, Birmingham and two one year posts in Ludlow and South London. I spent the next seven years working in Personnel (now Human Resources), first at Hammersmith Hospital and then at Imperial College.

Shortly after I came to London I settled in Earls Court and joined St Jude's, Courtfield Gardens. It was the early 70's, when the Charismatic movement was gathering strength. At St Jude's we were deeply affected and whole new spiritual horizons opened up for us. In 1974 we got the use of a disused pub on the Earls Court Road for a penny a month, and started evangelistic evenings – 9pm to 2am four nights a week. I described it afterwards as a time when "some people were converted to Christ, and the church was converted to the area".

In September 1977 some of us went on a weekend to the Post Green community, a charismatic lifestyle community in Dorset; it was there that, for no discernible reason, I realised I should join the community and then be ordained. So that is what I did. After two years at Post Green working in the Sales Department and the Pizza Parlour, I came back to Earls Court for a year and then did three years training at Durham, again a wonderful time of learning and friendship.

In 1984 I became curate at St Leonard's Streatham, and learnt liturgy from the gifted vicar, Jeffry Wilcox. I then became curate-in-charge at St John's Kingston for six years and experienced some of the ups and downs of parish life. In 1994 I became priest-in-charge of All Saints Hackbridge and stayed there for 21 years right up to my retirement. This probably only worked because in 2000 I married Linda, a lawyer in DEFRA

BRIEF

came a step-dad to Peter, then six. A couple of years later a friend commented how much marriage had improved me, and I believe them! In my time at All Saints I helped with a major restoration of our church community centre in 1994-6 and a refurbishment of the church itself including installing a toilet and kitchenette in 2014.

My leisure interests have been music - classical and folk, films, walking, and going on lovely holiday breaks with Linda.

I retired in 2015 and Linda and I moved to the flat in Earls Court I had bought in 1976. It is a vibrant community where I hope I can make my own contribution. As one of my cards said, "Retirement is a journey, not a destination".

One of my passions has always been to communicate the Christian faith in a way which is intelligible, whether by starting a community newspaper in Hackbridge, or by developing a simple five session course on the basic Christian story, using DVD's, the Bible and open discussion. My hope is that this book will help someone to discover for themselves what the Bible says in its varied voices, and to go on to explore for themselves "the light of the knowledge of the glory of God in the face of Christ". (2 Corinthians 3.18)

Bonus Featu